Modeling, Designing and Programming Database Applications

Relational, Entity-Relationship, SQL, DB and UI Programming

2nd Edition

Pedro Furtado

2015

DEDICATION

This book is dedicated to the most precious things in my life, my two children Pedro and Diogo. They helped me a lot, and they deserve all my help and support. It is also dedicated to all those who, like me, do not stop when facing difficulties. Hard honest work is always worth it.

CONTENTS AT A GLANCE

About the Author 1

List of Acronyms 3

List of Figures 5

Preface 7

1. Introduction 11

2. The Relational Data Model 17

3. Structured Query Lang. (SQL) 47

4. SQL Functions and Exercises 65

5. Entity-Relationship Model 85

6. Entity-Relationship to Relational 111

7. Design and Development 139

8. References 169

Pedro Furtado

TABLE OF CONTENTS

About the Author 1

List of Acronyms 3

List of Figures 5

Preface 7

1. Introduction 11

2. The Relational Data Model 17
   2.1. Relations 18
   2.2. Identifiers, References, Modification Anomalies and
   Normalization 23
   2.3. Constraints, Consistency and Integrity 29
   2.4. Identity Constraints and the Primary Key 30
   2.5. Referential Integrity and Foreign Keys 34
   2.6. Domain and Business Rule Constraints 37
   2.7. Handling Violations of Integrity Constraints 40
   2.8. Relational Algebra Operations and Extensions 41

3. Structured Query Lang. (SQL) 47
   3.1. SQL as a Programming Language 47
   3.2. Servers, Clients and SQL 50
   3.3. Data Definition Language (SQL-DDL) 50
   3.4. Data Manipulation Language (SQL-DML) 54
   3.5. Query Language (SQL-QL) and Query Clauses 56
   3.6. An Illustration of Query Operations Sequence 62

4. SQL Functions and Exercises 65
   4.1. Dummy Schema 65
   4.2. Tuple Functions and Operators 67
      4.2.1. String Functions 68
      4.2.2. Examples of Date Functions 69
      4.2.3. Examples of Arithmetic Functions 70
      4.2.4. Exercises 70
   4.3. Select, Project, Where and Order By 71

4.4. Join Operations...73

4.5. Cartesian Product, Union and Difference 75

4.6. Aggregations..76

4.6.1. Examples of Aggregation Functions.............................77

4.6.2. Exercises 77

4.7. Subqueries 79

4.7.1. Exercises 81

5. Entity-Relationship Model...85

5.1. Strength of Entity-Relationship Model........................86

**5.1. Entity-Relationship and Relational versus Object
Orientation** 87

5.2. Defining the Entity-Relationship Model.......................89

5.2.1. Example 1. A Database of Projects................................90

5.2.2. Example 2 - Food Factory Quality Control Database........97

5.2.3. Example 3. Clinical Information Database 101

5.3. Identifiers 102

5.4. Attributes..107

6. Entity-Relationship to Relational....................................111

6.1. R(e). Entity-to-Relation Default Transformation.............112

6.2. R(1:1). Transformations of 1:1 Relationships..................112

6.3. R(1:N). Transformations of 1:N Relationships.................116

6.4. R(N:M). Transformations of N:M Relationships 118

6.5. Rweak. Weak 1:N (and 1:1) Relationships......................120

6.6. RI. Inheritance Relationships..122

6.7. Complete ER-R Transformation Examples 129

6.7.1. Example 1. Projects Database 129

6.7.2. Example 2. Relational Food Quality Database 135

6.7.3. Example 3. Relational Model of Clinical Information 136

7. Design and Development...139

7.1. Phases and Paradigm for Design and Development..........139

7.2. Requirements and Use Cases...142

7.3. Prototyping and Designing User Interfaces 143

7.4. Some D&D Guidelines for Small Projects......................145

7.5. Using the Database: Console and Applications 147

7.6. Programming the User Interface 152

7.7.   **Importing and Exporting Data**..**164**

8.   **References** **169**

About the Author

Pedro Furtado is Professor at University of Coimbra UC, Portugal, where he teaches courses in both Computer and Biomedical Engineering. He has more than 25 years experience in both teaching, doing research and supervising industry projects. He has a broad interest in computer science subjects, with the main focus being on performance and scalability qualities of systems. Pedro applied these qualities in databases, data warehousing and analytics, bigdata, data mining, cloud, IoT and realtime systems. Pedro has more than 150 papers published in international conferences and journals, books published and several research collaborations with both industry and academia. In the last years, he has spent time as visiting scholar in some prestigious universities in the world, and collaborating with non-profit institutions.

Pedro Furtado

List of Acronyms

DBMS   Database Management System

RDBMS   Relational Database Management System

ER   Entity-Relationship Model

OLTP   Online Transactional Processing

OLAP   Online Analytical Processing

DW   Data Warehouse

Query   Question submitted to the RDBMS

SQL   Structured Query Language

API   Application Programming Interface

SE   Software Engineering

UI   User Interface

JDBC   Java Database Connectivity

UML   Unified Modeling Language

Prototype   Early model or piece of software to try and test future products

UI Prototype Prototype of the user interface, made as a drawing or a piece of software

UI Mockup Same as UI Prototype

Pedro Furtado

List of Figures

Figure 1 – Illustration of Structured and Unstructured Data   13

Figure 2. Example Relations (tables) for a Health Organism   19

Figure 3. Illustrating References: Patients, Doctors and Medical Procedure   24

Figure 4. Medical Procedure Diagram   25

Figure 5. The Universal Relation   26

Figure 6. Deletion Anomaly in Universal Relation   26

Figure 7. Insertion Anomaly in Universal Relation   27

Figure 8. Update Anomaly in Universal Relation   27

Figure 9. Patient and Medical Procedure Records with Wrong Reference   35

Figure 10. Data Types: Integer Numbers   38

Figure 11. Data Types: Other types   38

Figure 12. Sales Relation and Query Output   46

Figure 13. Illustrating Operations of Select-where Query   62

Figure 14. Illustrating Operations of Aggregation Query   63

Figure 15. Illustrating Operations of Join   64

Figure 16 – A Person with Children in an OO Model   87

Figure 17 – A Person with Children in ER model and as Relations   87

Figure 18. Project-Task Relationship arity: Alternatives   93

Figure 19. Task-Consultant Relationship   93

Figure 20. Draft Entity-Relationship Diagram for Projects Database   94

Figure 21. Examples of Mandatory and Optional Participation in Relationships
95

Figure 22. ER Diagram for Projects, with Arity and Optionality   97

Figure 23. ER Model of Food Factory Quality Control Database - I   100

Figure 24. ER Model of Food Factory Quality Control Database - II   100

Figure 25. ER Model for the Hospital Clinical Information Database   102

Figure 26. Entity-Relationship with Identifiers   104

Figure 27. Dependency Relationship   104

Figure 28. Projects Database – Relationship Attributes   105

Figure 29. Projects Database – M:N Relationship as weak Entity   106

Figure 30. Projects Database – completing an identifier to M:N Relationship
106

Figure 31. Projects Database - Customer Inheritance   107

Figure 32. Project-Customer part of the Projects Database ER   108

Figure 33. Refined Project-Customer part of the Projects Database ER   108

Figure 34. Project-Task-Consultant part of the Projects Database ER   *109*
Figure 35. Customer-Address (Mandatory) Example   *115*
Figure 36.Customer-Address (Optional) Example   *115*
Figure 37. Project-Task 1:N Relationship   *117*
Figure 38. Project-Task 1:N Optional Relationship   *118*
Figure 39. Supplier-Product M:N Example   *120*
Figure 40. Project-Task II: Dependent Entity and Relationship   *121*
Figure 41. Customer and its Inheritance Relationship   *123*
Figure 42. Customer Inheritance (P+C$_i$)   *123*
Figure 43. Customer inheritance (C$_i$)   *125*
Figure 44. Relational Model of alternative (P and C$_i$)   *126*
Figure 45. (P and C$_i$) Conceptual-to-conceptual Transformation   *128*
Figure 46. Relational Model of alternative (P and some C$_i$)   *129*
Figure 47. Relational Model of the Projects Database   *130*
Figure 48. Refined Relational Model of the Projects Database   *131*
Figure 49. Refined Relational Model of the Projects Database   *131*
Figure 50. Relational Model for Food Quality Control Database   *136*
Figure 51. Relational Model for the Clinical Information Database   *137*
Figure 52. Use Case for Module Login& Profile   *143*
Figure 53. Mockup of ATM Login Screen   *144*
Figure 54. Parts of a Data Application   *147*
Figure 55. Web Interactions for the Example Table a   *153*
Figure 56. Webpage auth.html   *154*
Figure 57. Output of auth.html Form   *154*

Preface

Dear reader,

The last years have seen exciting developments in the areas of Databases. When you book some travel, use ATM machines, buy something in a shop, pick some packet that arrived by mail, go to the bank, search for an apartment, make a legal registration of a new apartment you bought, or use the web, even when you open a newspaper, data management is always present in some related activity. This is because most human activities are systematically recorded and make use of data based information systems to help search, organize and manage. Your latest medical imaging records are also stored or indexed in a database.

As more and more of our daily lives became organized around computerized data, storing, querying and analyzing that data became important activities to allow organizations to work efficiently.

This book is a textbook that teaches the main tools you need in order to develop database applications, and makes you ready to investigate further on your own using the web and other resources. It is also a book that teaches you the most important rudiments of data management models, techniques and technologies, as well as data application development and data analysis. We provide the necessary basic information for anyone to become knowledgeable in using, creating and developing databases, database applications and in doing data analysis, discovering knowledge from the data. But, most importantly, we give the reader the initial jumpstart to search for more in-depth information on specialized issues.

What most sets this book apart from existing books on developing data applications, data management, and data analysis solutions is that it gives you the tools to work on your own data application project in a well-organized way, teaches you about the models, techniques and base technologies you need to know about, and at the same time takes a very practice-oriented perspective, focusing on concepts and examples that prepare you to use in practical applications.

The book starts by introducing the relational model, the logical organization in traditional databases used to store and organize data, using examples and giving you the tools to work on the subject. Then we describe the structured query language (SQL), the standard language that is used to query and manipulate data in databases, and prepare you to use it by means of examples and solved exercises. Next we present the entity-relationship (ER) conceptual data modeling approach. The approach is not presented as a theory, instead we organize the presentation with examples in such a way that the reader will be able to follow the steps to create actual models, and we convey an approach to arrive at a good ER model that we have refined along years. In the end we would like the reader to be able to design good new ER models for any applications from scratch. Complete illustrative examples are used to show how you should think when you design a database application. After the ER model is created, it must be translated into a relational model. We explain how this is done continuing the examples that we created for the ER model.

Database applications must be developed using some programming language that usually includes interaction with users and access to the database. We discuss applications programming, database connectors and user interface programming. Practical illustrative examples are provided. Many of today's user interfaces are web-based, others are based on rich data and user interface objects. For this reason, we included some basic information and examples related to programming data applications with those programming models. Although we include a lot of examples, all this information concerning the programming of data applications is intended only as a jumpstart for the reader to start programming data applications and to investigate further, since there are many details and different frameworks that can be used.

This book is adequate for undergraduate courses in databases and data analysis, or as a reference in undergraduate or graduate courses on databases and data analysis. It assumes no prerequisites, and is suitable for students with various backgrounds, from computer sciences to computer engineering, or other engineering disciplines.

Looking at the future, this book focuses on models, techniques and approach to develop data applications, and how to use Relational Database Management Systems (RDBMS). We see four obvious subjects that extend this knowledge into more specialized fields beyond the scope of this book: Application Programming, inside Database Management Systems, data Warehousing and Data Mining. The first subject is very framework dependent. For the other three, we also authored two other books to be published soon after this one. One is about how Database Management Systems (DBMS) are organized and how they can be made to scale. The second one is about Data Warehousing and Data Mining.

It is difficult to find books with similar content and teaching approach as this book, especially in what concerns modeling, designing and developing database applications and in what concerns the richness of examples. However, there exist many interesting complementary "further reading" books. In particular, readers seeking further knowledge concerning the details of database management systems can choose among the following references [5][6][7][8][9].

Pedro Furtado

1. Introduction

Data Management concerns how to organize, store, retrieve and search any kind of data in a computerized system. A **database** is a set of data, organized in some pre-defined structure. The World-wide-web (a.k.a. the Web) is an example of a huge database. As the name itself implies, search engines are mechanisms designed to search over the Web.

Database Management Systems (DBMS) are software applications that organize, store and search data. DBMS define how the data is physically organized (structure), how it is stored (storage mechanisms), how it is queried, deleted and updated physically. The term "physically" is very important here. It means that the DBMS defines the detailed computerized mechanisms that you do not need to know about in order to use. DBMS are designed for users that do not need to know how they work. Instead, interfaces are provided to interact with the data in the DBMS. It is just like when you drive a car, you do not need to know the physical details of how the car mechanisms work.

Data and **Information** are closely related concepts. It is common to consider data as being the raw, un-interpreted pieces of a content, while information is what you can extract from the data that is useful or knowledgeable. For instance, in a book, data is the detailed characters, words and numbers or symbols that we use to express all sorts of information. There is a spectrum of information representation that goes all the way from unstructured to completely structured. Unstructured data is data that has no discernable structure. Semi-structured data is data that has some structure, but is only partly-structured.

Structure is important for a computerized system to be able to retrieve data and derive information from it. While searching for some specific information in large stocks of unstructured or semi-structured data can be hard, if the data is stored in a structured manner from the start, such questions become trivial. Figure 1(a) shows an example of a semi-structured newspaper page, and Figure 1(b) shows a structured schema where data is stored in entities with predefined attributes. The newspaper page includes a graph with stock market data along time, and the structured schema represents the stock market data as a set of tables. It is difficult for a computerized application to find all companies that increased their revenue more than 25% in the last 5 years by looking at stocks represented in the online newspaper page. However, the following query retrieves the answer to that question instantly by searching over a structured schema similar to the one in Figure 1(b) and by using a specialized search language (SQL):

```
SELECT company
FROM
(select sum(revenue) as revenue, company
where year(date) = year(today)
from companyEarnings
group by company) as revenueNow,
(select sum(revenue) as revenue, company
where year(date) = year(today)-5 years
from companyEarnings
group by company) as revenue5
JOIN revenuewNow TO revenue5 ON company
WHERE          (revenueNow.revenue-revenue5.revenue)          /
revenue5.revenue>0.25
```

(a) Semi-structured data

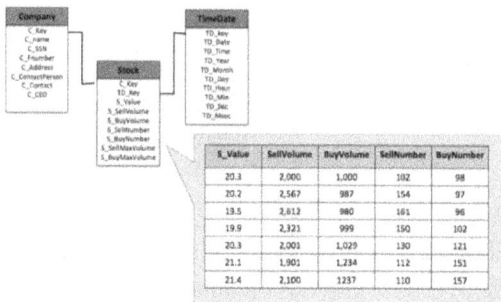

(b) Structured Data

Figure 1 – Illustration of Structured and Unstructured Data

Both kinds of data (structured, semi-structured and unstructured) are important. Unstructured or semi-structured data is the means that most people use to convey information in everyday life.

Structuring the data requires extensive work to create the structure, to format the data and to insert it into a database. The data is usually structured to meet specific data management and/or data analysis objectives, and the same data frequently coexists in structured and less structured representations. For instance, summaries of stock market data are printed in a newspaper for readers, while the same data also coexists in structured organization in a database of stock values.

Coming back to the concept of Database and Database Management Systems (DBMS), a database is a collection of data using some storage organization, and a DBMS is a collection of programs that enables to store, modify, and extract information from a database. There are different types of DBMS, from small DBMS that run on individual PCs, to DBMS running on servers and serving many users.

This book teaches how to design and query a structured database, and also the basics of how to develop applications and user interfaces using the databases that you have built. The following are examples of applications of databases that are used everyday: Management software is used in medium and large companies to record and manage all kinds of information, including for instance sales, customers, employees, accounting, inventories, projects, assets; Hospital Information Systems record and manage information about patients, clinical data, imaging, inventories, staff and many other data; Electronic Commerce websites store and manage information about sales, products, product catalogs; Banks have sophisticated databases that record every transaction and balance; Automated Teller Machines (ATMs) access bank databases remotely to authorize and to record transactions; You can book hotels, cars and flights over the internet thanks to the databases and search capabilities of the companies that sell those services; Travel agencies also access databases to book your trips; Airports and airline companies are fully computerized, so that flights can be booked and all kind of operations happen over their databases.

A database query is a request for information submitted in the form of a Structured Query. We already saw a complex query before. It is important for the database query language to be both declarative (users specify what they want, not the complex instructions that a machine needs to retrieve the answer), and universal (different DBMS should support the same query language). That is why the Structured Query Language (SQL) was created and adopted as a standard. It was designed to allow users to pose any query using a language that would be simple to understand by humans and interpretable by the computer. SQL established a mechanism for interaction with the database system. The language is sufficiently intuitive for users to find out how to express their queries using it. For instance, if I want all information about every person named 'Smith' and who is more than 35 years old, it is enough to submit the query 'SELECT * FROM People WHERE name = "Smith" AND age> 35.

It is easy to make "poor design" choices when creating the structure of a database, which is called the schema. For instance, in the example above there is a subtle "poor design" feature in the database that supports the query. The field "age" is mutant along time. Each person changes his age every year. This means that the age field would have to be updated for each person every year on a specific birthday date, and this should be done automatically. Instead of the field "age", it would have been better to have a field "birthdate" that is not mutant. The new query would be 'SELECT * FROM People WHERE name = "Smith" AND birthdate< today – 35 years.

In the next chapters we teach how to build databases, how to interact with them, and how to build database applications and their user interfaces. The emphasis is on providing examples and the tools for the reader to be able to build databases correctly, and to give the reader a jumpstart in what concerns application development.

Pedro Furtado

2. The Relational Data Model

This chapter introduces the relational model and discusses how it is used in database applications. We describe relations, identifiers, references, modification anomalies and normalization. Then we discuss integrity constraints and how applications should handle violations of those integrity constraints. Finally, we discuss operations on relations, relational algebra and extensions to relational algebra that are used in R-DBMS.

When using the relational model in practical applications, data is represented in a relational schema that is stored in a computer (the server) by a relational database management system (R-DBMS). The R-DBMS is a software product that manages relational databases in the server. One or more applications offer user interfaces for users to interact with the database, either locally or remotely. Based on requests by the user, the application interacts with the database by submitting requests to the R-DBMS, receiving responses from it and formatting the data to present results to the user.

2.1. Relations

The foundations of relational databases is relational algebra, as defined by Codd [1], and derived from set theory. Set theory is a well-known mathematical theory of sets. Sets are collections of objects (members or elements). According to set theory axioms, all mathematical objects can be built as sets. Given an object o (the object can be a set itself) and a set S, the object is a member or element of the set if the membership relation o ∈ S holds. Given sets A and B, the inclusion relation holds iff A ⊆ B. Set theory also defines a set of well-known binary operations on sets, including Intersection, Union, Set Difference, Cartesian Product. The Cartesian Product is a set whose members are all possible ordered pairs of members from the two sets participating in the operation.

Relational algebra is based in set theory and defines the same operations on relations. Data is represented as sets of tuples, and the sets are called relations.

Definition 1. **Tuple** (T) – A tuple can be defined as a set of predicates on attributes that are associated with the tuple. It can also be defined as a set of values taken by the attributes that are associated with the tuple.

Definition 2. **Relation** (R) and **Relational Algebra** – A relation R is a set of tuples $R = \{tu_i\}$. The order of the tuples in the set is unimportant. Relational algebra operations apply to the relations. In those operations, the sets are the relations and the members of the sets are the tuples.

Definition 3. **Table** (T), **Attributes, Rows**– A table is the representation of a relation in a relational database. It is a two-dimensional object, with columns and rows. A table has a unique name and a set of columns, which are the attributes of the relation. The rows of the table are tuples of the relation. For each row (tuple), attributes can take one value from a domain defined for the attribute. Rows can be in any order (order is not important), and the order of the attributes in the columns of the table is also not important.

From now on we will use the terms relation and table indistinguishably when we discuss the relational model and/or R-DBMS, and we also use the terms tuple and row interchangeably.

Figure 2 shows three relations (tables), Patient, Physician and Procedure. These relations store information about the patients, medical doctors and procedures that are scheduled in some hospital.

Attributes, Data Types and Domains: Looking at the Patient relation, its attributes are (Patient ID, First Name, Middle Initial, Last Name, Address, City, Zip Code, Country, Phone Number and Date of Birth). Each attribute has a domain, which is the set of values that it can take. For instance, the domain of 'Patient ID' could be N, the set of natural numbers. The domain of attribute 'Country' could be defined by extension, as the set of countries in the world.

Patient (Person)

Patient ID	First Name	Middle Initial	Last Name	Address	City	Zip Code	Country	Phone Number	Date of Birth
19845	Joaquim	N.	Gomes	Rua Castilho, 23	Lisboa	2720-234	Portugal	91-99893	2/10/00
21537	Manuel	M.	Silva	Rua Augusta, 18	Coimbra	3000-542	Portugal	96-39494	2/10/90
82435	Victor	P.	Correira	Rua da Prata	Lisboa	2453-122	Portugal	21-789876	1/9/87

Physician(Person)

Physician ID	First Name	Middle Initial	Last Name	Address	City	Zip Code	Country	Phone Number	Date of Birth
11	Jorge	S.	Matos	Rua das Laranjeiras	Lisboa	2100-131	Portugal	91-614528	28499
12	Paulo	J.	Martins	Rua do Olival	Lisboa	2100-231	Portugal	91-548722	31082

(a) Person records

Procedure

Patient	Symptoms	Diagnosis	Physician	Physician Phone Number	Already Scheduled?	Schedule
Joaquim Gomes	Accute headache	Concussion	Dr. Martins	91-548722	yes	20/6/2015, 10:00
Manuel Silva	Sharp pain in lower abdomen	Food poisoning	Dr. Matos	91-614528	no	-

(b) Procedure records

Figure 2. Example Relations (tables) for a Health Organism

How do we create a table in SQL? The Patient relation of Figure 2 can be expressed in pseudo-SQL very easily as shown in Algorithm 1.

This simple command creates the table, specifying attribute names and domains. A varchar(s) is a variable sized array of characters (String) with the specification of its maximum size s.

```
CREATE TABLE Patient(
PatientID integer,
FirstName varchar(50),
MiddleInitial varchar(50),
LastName varchar(50),
Address varchar(100),
City varchar(50),
ZipCode varchar(10),
Country String varchar(50),
PhoneNumber varchar(14),
DateOfBirth Date);
```
Algorithm 1. Pseudo SQL code to create Patients table

A Data Type is a set. Examples of pre-defined sets are N (natural numbers), Z (integer numbers), R (real numbers), Strings, Dates. Database Management Systems and Programming Languages define specific data types, while standards such as SQL define a set of data types that systems complying with the standard need to support.

The Domain of an attribute is defined as a data type and a set of constraints on the data type, which restricts the values that the attribute can take in the set. The constraints can be defined in varied ways. One approach is to list the admissible values by enumeration (e.g. country can be Portugal, France, …); another is to define constraint predicates (e.g. birthdate>0, salary>0 and salary <20000).

It is frequent for students to ask what data type some attributes should take. For instance, can the field PatientID be a string, or does it need to be an integer? Does the DateOfBirth need to be a Date, or can it be a String?

When answering such questions we should consider functionality, constraints and, in some (rare) cases also performance. Consider date attributes. Could we use a String to represent a date? We should not allow invalid dates to be inserted into the database, and we should be able to use simple functions that are already provided to determine how many years, months or days have gone by since a certain date. Those are the reasons why we should use a Date data type for dates.

In what concerns the PatientID attribute, could it be a String, or should it be a numeric field? We do not need to do any computations with it, since it is only an identifier, with no numeric meaning besides being an identifier. If we needed to sum, compute the difference or other arithmetic operations with the attribute, that would be a strong argument in favor of having it as a number. However, we still need to increment PatientID to guarantee that it is unique, and checking whether it is unique is probably faster as an integer than if it was a string. Those are arguments in favor of using an integer number representation for the attribute PatientID instead of a String, although it could be represented as a String.

Constraints: In order to avoid errors in the representation of data – wrong data, duplications, misspellings – it is necessary to enforce constraints on the data that is stored. For instance, Patient names can be constrained to start by capital letter and have the remaining letters in lowercase; phone numbers should have two to three prefix digits, followed by a hyphen and a set of 5 digits; The country should be chosen from an enumeration of countries, instead of allowing any arbitrary string to be entered; The birthdate should have a format 'dd/mm/yyyy'.

If we do not enforce the constraint defined above on admissible patient names, perhaps we could end up with the person 'Joaquim Gomes' appearing also as 'JOAQUIM GOMES' and 'joaquim gomes'.

This raises another issue, that a database application should guarantee that a specific instance of an entity should appear only once in the entity (e.g. a specific person should appear only once in the Patient relation). When or before inserting a new person, it should be checked whether that person is already represented in the database, and in that case, it should not be inserted again. Uniqueness is enforced by adding a UNIQUE constraint to an attribute that cannot have repeated values. For example, uniqueness of persons can be enforced by defining an 'ID Card Number' field, with a UNIQUE constraint. The DBMS always checks that no two tuples can have the same value for an attribute that was defined as UNIQUE.

Tuples as constraints: as we already indicated, a relation is defined as a set of tuples, and a tuple is a set of values, one for each attribute of a set of attributes. In the Patients and Medical Procedures example, tuples are an individual patient or a specific record of a medical procedure. As a curiosity from relational algebra, note that a tuple can be defined as a predicate that is a conjunction of predicates on individual attributes. For instance, patient 'Joaquim Gomes' is well-represented as a predicate as,

Patient ID=19845 AND First Name=' Joaquim'
AND Middle Initial='N.' AND Last Name='Gomes'
AND Address=' Rua Castilho, 23' AND City='Lisboa'
AND Zip Code='2720-234' AND Country='Portugal'
AND Phone Number='91-99893' AND Date Of Birth='2/10/00'

Atomicity: the relational model requires attribute values to be atomic. This means that each attribute of a tuple must be assigned a single value. For instance, the 'Phone Number' attribute should be a single String, it cannot be a set of Strings. It would not be possible to have an attribute 'Phone Numbers'={'91-99893', '96-49792'}. We can have more than one phone number represented in the same attribute, but in a single String as in 'Phone Numbers'='91-99893, 96-49792'. However, this could be a bad design choice if we need to see if a specific number is in the database, or to search quickly by phone number. In order to find a specific phone number in the database, we would need to parse the values of the attribute 'Phone Numbers' in all tuples of the relation.

Order: the order of attributes and the order of tuples in a relation have no special meaning. Tuples and attributes in relations are unordered. It means that, if you change the order of tuples or attributes in a relation, you will still have the same relation.

A short representation of a relation is $R = \{ tu_i\{a_{ij} : v_{ij}\} \}$. In this representation, tu_i denotes a tuple, $\{\}$ denotes set, a_{ij} denotes an attribute and v_{ij} denotes the value of attribute a_{ij} in tuple tu_i. Since tuples can also be represented as predicates, the relation R can also be represented as a conjunction of predicates, $R = \{ \text{AND pred}_i\{a_{ij}:v_{ij}\} \}$.

Defined: In the relational model, an attribute cannot have an undefined value. This is limitation of the model, since it constrains what can be represented. We can see this in the predicate representation of a tuple. The tuple,

<Patient ID=19845 AND First Name=' Joaquim'
AND Middle Initial='N.' AND Last Name='Gomes'
AND Address=' Rua Castilho, 23' AND **City='Lisboa'**
AND Zip Code='2720-234' AND Country='Portugal'
AND Phone Number='91-99893' AND Date Of Birth='2/10/00'>

represents a specific person living in the city of Lisboa, whereas the forbidden tuple:

< Last Name='Gomes' AND Country='Portugal' >

would represent all people with last name 'Gomes' living in Portugal. Such tuple is forbidden, since it has undefined values for all attributes that are not represented in the conjunction predicate.

This is a major limitation of the relational model, and a reason for the development of alternative models, such as constraint databases.

2.2. Identifiers, References, Modification Anomalies and Normalization

The relational model defines relations, holding data, and references from one relation to another. Each tuple is required to have a unique identifying attribute or set of attributes that is called the primary key. The attributes PatientID and PhysicianID are examples of unique identifiers.

In the example shown previously in Figure 2 there was a reference from Medical Procedure to Patient, and another from Medical Procedure to Medical Doctor. Those references can be defined as 'Patient X

undergoes a medical procedure', and 'Doctor Y **is assigned** the medical procedure'. We know which patient undergoes the medical procedure because relation Procedure in Figure 2 includes the name of the patient in the medical procedure record. Similarly, Procedure also includes the name of the doctor.

Although we used the names of patients and medical doctors as references, external references from one tuple to another should preferably be tuples identifiers. Figure 3 represents the same relational schema as Figure 2, but references in table Procedure to tables Patient and Doctor are based on attributes PatientID and PhysicianID of the respective tables, instead of names of the persons. For instance, Patient 19845 in table 'Procedure' is 'Joaquim Gomes' in table Patient, since the PatientID is the same as the value of attribute Patient in table 'Procedure'.

Patient (Person)

Patient ID	First Name	Middle Initial	Last Name	Address	City	Zip Code	Country	Phone Number	Date of Birth
19845	Joaquim	N.	Gomes	ua Castilho, 2	Lisboa	2720-234	Portugal	91-99893	2/10/00
21537	Manuel	M.	Silva	ua Augusta, 1	Coimbra	3000-542	Portugal	96-39494	2/10/90
82435	Victor	P.	Correira	Rua da Prata	Lisboa	2453-122	Portugal	21-789876	1/9/87

Physician(Person)

Physician ID	First Name	Middle Initial	Last Name	Address	City	Zip Code	Country	Phone Number	Date of Birth
11	Jorge	S.	Matos	a das Laranjei	Lisboa	2100-131	Portugal	91-614528	28499
12	Paulo	J.	Martins	Rua do Olival	Lisboa	2100-231	Portugal	91-548722	31082

Procedure

Patient	Symptoms	Diagnosis	Physician	Already Scheduled?	Schedule
19845	Accute headache	Concussion	12	yes	20/6/2015, 10:00
21537	Sharp pain in lower abdomen	Food poisoning	11	no	-

Figure 3. Illustrating References: Patients, Doctors and Medical Procedure

Figure 4 is another possible representation of the relations and references involved in the example, showing that patients undergo medical procedures, and doctors are assigned medical procedures. It conveys a lot less information, since it depicts only relation names, references and reference labels. But it allows us to analyze the design without being distracted by details. Both diagrams of Figure 3 and Figure 4 are important tools during design and analysis of the design.

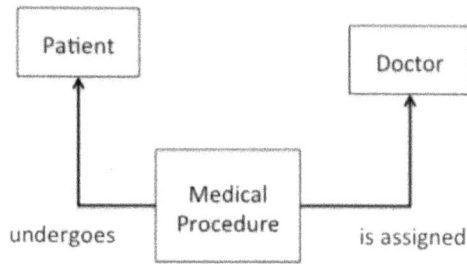

Figure 4. Medical Procedure Diagram

Another important issue when talking about the relational model is normalization. Relational databases and normalization were first defined in [1] and the second and third normal forms, which are outcomes of normalizing a schema, were defined in [2].

Imagine a single big relation containing all data from all entities. This is called a universal relation. If the relation 'Medical Procedure' would store all the data about medical procedures, including patients undergoing the procedures and doctors doing the procedures, a lot of redundancy and anomalies could happen. For instance, if doctor X did 5,000 procedures, all the information about X would be repeated 5,000 times. On the contrary, a normalized schema is a schema consisting of multiple relations and references between the relations such that all redundancy is eliminated. Normalization is the process followed to obtain a normalized schema, one that should have no unwanted redundancy or anomalies.

Figure 5 shows a single big relation with the attributes of the medical procedure and the patient. We should have included also data about the medical doctor, but it would be too big to represent in this page.

It is easy to see why redundancy may happen in the universal relation. Since a patient may undergo more that one medical procedure (even during the same hospital visit), we will have more than one tuple with all data about the same patient, such as his home address. Similarly, if we had the data bout the medical doctor as well, we would repeat all data about a specific doctor tens of thousands of times, since he does many medical procedures.

First Name	Middle Initial	Last Name	Address	City	Zip Code	Country	Phone Number	Date of Birth	PatientID	Symptoms	Diagnosis	Already Scheduled?	Schedule
Joaquim	N.	Gomes	Rua Castilho, 23	Lisboa	2720-234	Portugal	91-99893	2/10/00	19845	Accute headache	Concussion	yes	20/6/2015, 10:00
Manuel	M.	Silva	Rua Augusta, 18	Coimbra	3000-542	Portugal	96-39494	2/10/90	21537	Sharp pain in lower abdomen	Food poisoning	no	.

Figure 5. The Universal Relation

Three types of modification anomalies can happen when we have a single de-normalized relation like the one in Figure 5.

A deletion anomaly happens when we want to delete one instance of an entity. In the relational model, we cannot delete only part of a tuple. If we delete a medical procedure, but that medical procedure is the only procedure registered for one specific patient, we also loose all information about the patient. This is what happens in the example of Figure 6, where we delete one medical procedure that was done on patient 'Joaquim Gomes', loosing all information about that patient as well.

First Name	Middle Initial	Last Name	Address	City	Zip Code	Country	Phone Number	Date of Birth	PatientID	Symptoms	Diagnosis	Already Scheduled?	Schedule
Joaquim	N.	Gomes	Rua Castilho, 23	Lisboa	2720-234	Portugal	91-99893	2/10/00	19845	Accute headache	Concussion	yes	20/6/2015, 10:00
Manuel	M.	Silva	Rua Augusta, 18	Coimbra	3000-542	Portugal	96-39494	2/10/90	21537	Sharp pain in lower abdomen	Food poisoning	no	.

Figure 6. Deletion Anomaly in Universal Relation

An insertion anomaly happens when we insert new data. Figure 7 shows what happens when we insert a new row into the universal relation 'Medical Procedure'. We cannot insert only information of a single entity (patient or medical procedure), unless we allow values to be null in all fields of the other entity. In a hospital registry system, the patient data could be inserted into the database as he arrives in the medical unit, while information on medical procedures is inserted only later. Furthermore, there is a many-to-one relationship between medical procedures and patients (multiple medical procedures can be added for a patient). This introduces redundancy. In Figure 7 there are two complete records representing the same instance of entity Patient, the patient 'Joaquim Gomes'. This is undesirable, as every change in one tuple of that instance must be replicated into all other copies of the same instance.

Insertion
Anomaly

First Name	Middle Initial	Last Name	Address	City	Zip Code	Country	Phone Number	Date of Birth	PatientID	Symptoms	Diagnosis	Already Scheduled?	Schedule
Joaquim	N.	Gomes	Rua Castilho, 23	Lisboa	2720-234	Portugal	91-99893	2/10/00	19845	Accute headache	Concussion	yes	20/6/2015, 10:00
Manuel	M.	Silva	Rua Augusta, 18	Coimbra	3000-542	Portugal	96-39494	2/10/90	21537	Sharp pain in lower abdomen	Food poisoning	no	-
Joaquim	N.	Gomes	Rua Castilho, 23	Lisboa	2720-234	Portugal	91-99893	2/10/00	19845	Pain in the mouth	Dental abscess	no	-

Figure 7. Insertion Anomaly in Universal Relation

The update anomaly illustrated in Figure 8 consists of changing attribute values of one instance of 'Joaquim Gomes'. The relation is left in an inconsistent state, since more than one tuple represents the same patient instance with different values of some attributes (address, city and zip code in the example). The database will give inconsistent answers to queries for the address of the person.

Modification
Anomaly

First Name	Middle Initial	Last Name	Address	City	Zip Code	Country	Phone Number	Date of Birth	PatientID	Symptoms	Diagnosis	Already Scheduled?	Schedule
Joaquim	N.	Gomes	Rua Murão, 2	Coimbra	3000-210	Portugal	91-99893	2/10/00	19845	Accute headache	Concussion	yes	20/6/2015, 10:00
Manuel	M.	Silva	Rua Augusta, 18	Coimbra	3000-542	Portugal	96-39494	2/10/90	21537	Sharp pain in lower abdomen	Food poisoning	no	-
Joaquim	N.	Gomes	Rua Castilho, 23	Lisboa	2720-234	Portugal	91-99893	2/10/00	19845	Pain in the mouth	Dental abscess	no	-

Figure 8. Update Anomaly in Universal Relation

How should a database designer avoid the universal relation (fully de-normalized schema) to create a schema with multiple relations and references between them (normalized schema)? Although detailed procedures to normalize to the 2nd, 3rd and other normal forms were defined by others, based on analyzing dependencies between individual attributes, we favor always using an Entity-Relationship (ER) modeling approach that we describe in a later chapter, with a top-down procedure based on identifying entities and relationships such that a simple normalization-check rule is verified. Next we present the normalization-check rule that should be part of your analysis while using an ER modeling approach.

The approach involves identifying entities in the problem domain that correspond to independent real-world entities and obey to the normalization-check rule. The rule is that, for the intended applications that will use the schema, all insertion or removal operations affect a single entity entirely:

"All insertion or removal operations that affect an entity must involve all attributes of that entity (no insertion or removal can affect only some attributes), none of the attributes affected by such operations can belong to another entity, and no attribute of other entities should be affected."

For instance, a patient is an independent real-world entity with a set of attributes identifying him and indicating where he lives. A medical procedure is the registry of what is done to a patient. It needs to be represented as an independent entity from patient, since we can have for instance patients without procedures (patient registry) and multiple procedures for a patient. If we need to delete a tuple of a medical procedure for some reason, we should not have to remove patient data. Medical Doctors are another independent entity. They are inserted into the database when they start working in the hospital, and they participate in huge numbers of medical procedures along their working life.

When we identify entities and check the rule, we are implicitly defining the dependencies that lead to normalization, and we are normalizing the schema.

The identification of independent entities and rule checking is just part of the more elaborate Entity-Relationship (ER) data modeling approach that we will describe in a later chapter. In ER modeling, it is necessary to identify independent entities, relationships and degree or cardinality of the relationships. One entity may have one-to-one, many-to-one or one-to-many relationships with other entities. Entities are most often assigned separate relations when transforming into the relational model, and this is mandatory in one-to-many and many-to-one relationships. We also need to identify attributes, and when we test the normalization check rule with those attributes we may detect problems and need to redesign the entities. For instance, while we are analyzing Medical Procedure, we may discover that we should include information about diagnostic exams that patients undergo. Such information may be independent from hospital visits and lead us to add an independent entity.

2.3. Constraints, Consistency and Integrity

The content of a database is consistent if it represents real-world entities and relationships accurately. If for instance one person, 'Joaquim Gomes', is represented twice in the Patient entity, the database is inconsistent. In the real-world, there is only one 'Joaquim Gomes', therefore we should have a single instance in the database. Another example is a salary of -2,000 €. Since salaries only take positive values, the database would be inconsistent. Integrity constraints are constraints that are created to help enforce consistency.

We can distinguish tuple consistency from consistency between tuples. Consistency between tuples is violated if two tuples represent the same item (violation of identity integrity), or when a tuple contains a reference to another tuple that does not exist (referential integrity). Consistency of individual tuples is related to following integrity constraints specified for the attributes of the tuple. For instance, attribute salary must be positive or zero (salary >=0). A birthdate of an employee cannot be in the future. These are called domain integrity constraints. The set of values that an attribute can take (the domain) can be defined as a set of integrity constraints. For instance, if the minimum wage is defined as 700€, the attribute salary can be defined as 'salary' ∈ ℕ | 'salary'>700.

Integrity constraints that need to be enforced are classified into the following groups that we describe in the next sections: identity, referential, domain, business rules and other integrity constraints.

2.4. Identity Constraints and the Primary Key

The identity constraint enforces the rule that any tuple must be uniquely identifiable by a subset of its attribute values. This also means that two tuples of a relation should not have exactly the same values in each attribute.

In general, the RDBMS does not forbid two distinct tuples of the same relation to take the same values. After we create relation Patient shown in Figure 2 using the command given in Algorithm 1, it is possible to insert the same row twice, thus violating this integrity constraint. For instance, we can issue the following command twice,

Insert into Patient values(19845,'Joaquim', 'N.', 'Gomes', 'Rua Castilho, 23', 'Lisboa', '2720-234','Portugal', '91-99893', '2/10/2000');

However, we can prevent those "duplicate tuples" By specifying a primary key. The primary key is a set of attributes that identifies tuples uniquely in a relation. Given a set PK=$\{a_i, ...,a_j\}$, named the primary key, PK is such that no two distinct tuples can have the same values for attributes $\{a_i, ...,a_j\}$. If tuple t1 has values $\{v_{i1}, ...,v_{j1}\}$ and tuple t2 has values $\{v_{i2}, ...,v_{j2}\}$ for the set of attributes $\{a_i, ...,a_j\}$, the following predicate must be true (!= means different): $v_{i1} != v_{i2}$ AND ... AND $v_{j1} != v_{j2}$.

The primary key must alo be "minimal". Being "Minimal" means that if a set of attributes$\{a_i, ...,a_j\}$ identifies tuples uniquely in a relation, no superset of attributes (e.g. $\{a_i, ...,a_j,a_{j+1}\}$) can be defined as a primary key.

A relation may have many candidate primary keys, defined as minimal sets of attributes that identify the tuples in the relation uniquely. Each possible primary key is named a 'Candidate Key', and the primary key is chosen from all candidate keys. Consider relation Person defined with the following attributes,

'Person' = { 'First Name', 'Last Name', 'Address', 'City', 'Country', 'Date of Birth' }

If we assume that there are no two persons with the same first and last names, then we can define the candidate key {'First Name', 'Last Name'}. Another candidate key could be {'Last Name', 'Address', 'Date of Birth'}, if we assume that there are no two persons with the same last name, address and date of birth. But if {'Last Name', 'Address' } is unique (no two different persons have the same values for those attributes in the relation), then the set {'Last Name', 'Address', 'Date of Birth'} should not be a candidate key, since it is not minimal.

The definition of a primary key is not applied to the tuples currently in the table, it applies to all tuples that may be inserted. If we define {'First Name', 'Last Name'} as a primary key, for all possible past, present or future tuples, no two tuples can have the same combination of values for these attributes.

Creating a primary key in SLQ is simple. It can be done while building the table, or as a solo command:

CREATE TABLE Person(
FirstName varchar(50),
MiddleInitial varchar(50),
LastName varchar(50),
Address varchar(100),
City varchar(50),
ZipCode varchar(10),
Country String varchar(50),
PhoneNumber varchar(14),
DateOfBirth Date,
PRIMARY KEY (FirstName, LastName));
          (a) Table creation with Primary Key

ALTER TABLE Person ADD PRIMARY KEY(FirstName, LastName);
          (b) Alternative Primary Key command format
Algorithm 2. Pseudo SQL for Primary Keys

It is possible to define 'natural' or 'artificial' primary keys. 'Natural primary keys' are sets of one or more attributes chosen from the relation that identify tuples uniquely. By contrast, an artificial primary key is an attribute created explicitly as a primary key, therefore it must be unique for all tuples.

```
CREATE TABLE Person(
PersonID integer PRIMARY KEY,
FirstName varchar(50),
MiddleInitial varchar(50),
LastName varchar(50),
Address varchar(100),
City varchar(50),
ZipCode varchar(10),
Country String varchar(50),
PhoneNumber varchar(14),
DateOfBirth Date);
```
Algorithm 3. Pseudo SQL code for artificial primary key

The attribute PersonID is artificial. Its only role is to provide a unique value for each distinct tuple in the table. The best implementation of an artificial primary ley is as a counter that increments automatically the value for each insert. There are more than one way to do that in modern DBMS, also depending on the specific DBMS. The attribute can be defined with a special domain that identifies an automatically incrementing value. To do that, just replace "PersonID integer PRIMARY KEY" in Algorithm 3 by "PersonID Serial PRIMARY KEY". Using the Serial keyword in the create table statement we afterwards insert new tuples into Person without specifying the serial attribute, since a value will be assigned to it automatically,

```
INSERT INTO Patient VALUES
( 'Joaquim', 'N.', 'Gomes', 'Rua Castilho, 23', 'Lisboa', '2720-234',
'Portugal', '91-99893', '2/10/2000');
```

If this is the first insert, then PersonID will be filled with value 1 automatically; If it is the second insert, it will take the value 2, and so on.

There is also no problem when we remove tuples from the relation. If for instance, we remove tuple with PersonID 2, that will not change anything in the assignment of PersonID from the serial attribute. The "Serial" keyword means that PersonID will always be incremented by one in the next insert from the current value of the counter (which is 2). This guarantees uniqueness of tuples. If we had two tuples with PersonID 1 and 2, removed the one with PersonID 2 and inserted a new tuple, the relation will end up with two tuples with values 1 and 3 for the attribute PersonID.

There is another approach defined in the SQL standard to have artificial primary keys generated automatically. The approach is based on sequences. A sequence is defined as,

CREATE SEQUENCE personID;

Now we use the functions nextval() and curval() to retrieve the next incremental value and the current value of the sequence. The relation would be defined as before, with no special syntax using the sequence (Algorithm 3), while the insert commands would use the sequence to guarantee unique values using the syntax shown next,

INSERT INTO Person VALUES
(**personID.nextval()**, 'Joaquim', 'N.', 'Gomes', 'Rua Castilho, 23', 'Lisboa', '2720-234','Portugal', '91-99893 ', '2/10/2000');

You can also view the current value of the sequence using the command "select personID.curval()".

Note that sequence creation commands support a lot of other optional parameters for indicating a starting value, the increment and many other options.

In many cases there is a natural key that is actually used as a unique identifier in the "real world". It is a natural key for this database, but it was created somewhere else to identify the items uniquely. For instance, in everyday life, different persons are distinguished by their identity card number, and different cars are distinguished by the license plate. In the Person table, it is a god idea to use the identity card number as the primary key, and forget about other candidate and artificial keys,

```
CREATE TABLE Person(
IdentityCardID Numeric(12) PRIMARY KEY,
FirstName varchar(50),
MiddleInitial varchar(50),
LastName varchar(50),
Address varchar(100),
City varchar(50),
ZipCode varchar(10),
Country String varchar(50),
PhoneNumber varchar(14),
DateOfBirth Date);
```
Algorithm 4. Pseudo SQL code to create table with primary key

The primary key must be unique and not null. Being unique means that it must have a unique value for any tuple of the relation. Being not-null means there cannot be any tuples with null value for the primary key.

2.5. Referential Integrity and Foreign Keys

Referential integrity concerns relationships (references) from one relation to another. In Figure 4 every medical procedure must be related with a patient. The reference 'undergoes' must have a valid patient ID and be associated with a specific medical procedure.

Figure 9 shows an example of a reference to a non-existent tuple of another relation. The 'Procedure' relation references patient 21343, which does not exist. This is a forbidden violation of a referential integrity constraint.

Patient ID	First Name	Middle Initial	Last Name	Address	City	Zip Code	Country	Phone Number	Date of Birth
19845	Joaquim	N.	Gomes	Rua Castilho, 23	Lisboa	2720-234	Portugal	91-99893	2/10/00
21537	Manuel	M.	Silva	Rua Augusta, 18	Coimbra	3000-542	Portugal	96-39494	2/10/90
82435	Victor	P.	Correira	Rua da Prata	Lisboa	2453-122	Portugal	21-789876	1/9/87

Patient (Person)

Procedure

Patient	Symptoms	Diagnosis	Physician	Physician Phone Number	Already Scheduled?	Schedule
21343	Accute headache	Concussion	12	91-548722	yes	20/6/2015, 10:00
21537	Sharp pain in lower abdomen	Food poisoning	11	91-614528	no	-

Figure 9. Patient and Medical Procedure Records with Wrong Reference

Foreign keys serve the purpose of guaranteeing the consistency of references. Algorithm 5 shows the creation of foreign keys for table MedicalProcedure, either embedded in the create table command itself or as a separate command.

CREATE TABLE MedicalProcedure(
Patient   Numeric(12)
                REFERENCES Patient(PatientID),
Symptoms   varchar(100),
Diagnosis   varchar(100),
Physician   Numeric(12)
                REFERENCES Doctor(DoctorID),
PhysicianPhoneNumber varchar(12),
AlreadyScheduled boolean,
Schedule   datetime);
(a) Table creation with Foreign Key

ALTER TABLE MedicalProcedure
CREATE FOREIGN KEY PatientFK REFERENCES Patient(PatientID);
(b) Separate Foreign Key creation command

ALTER TABLE table1
CREATE FOREIGN KEY compositeFK
REFERENCES table2(attr1, attr2);
(c) Composite Foreign Key Template

Algorithm 5. Alternatives for Creation of Foreign Keys

The foreign key is the referential integrity constraint that enforces referential integrity automatically. Any insert command that tries to insert data into a relation, such that the tuple to be inserted includes an invalid reference to another entity, results in an exception returned to the submitter. It also means that we cannot delete a tuple from a relation without previously deleting all tuples in other relations that refer to that tuple. Otherwise we would end up with inconsistent data that violates the referential integrity constraint.

We now denote as dependent the relation that has a foreign key to some other relation. Consider the case when we export data from a database schema into some files and upload those into another clone database schema. Bulk loading refers to loading the schema using data that is in files. The referential integrity enforcement rule does forbids loading tuples of dependent relations before loading the relations they refer to. The consequence of this is that there must be a careful order in bulk loading.

Given the enforcement of referential integrity constraints, there is also a problem when inserting data into two relations (A and B) where each references attributes of the other. Consider, for instance, the case that attribute A.a refers to attribute B.b, and attribute B.c references attribute A.d (a special case is B.c = B.b and A.d = A.a). There is no insertion order that works now, since one of the two referential integrity constraints would be violated. In order to avoid this, we can either create only one of the foreign keys, or disable one of the foreign keys prior to insertion, habilitating it again after insertion.

Foreign keys are not mandatory. They exist precisely to enforce referential integrity, but referential integrity can be enforced 'manually', meaning that the application code can verify the integrity each time it needs to insert, delete or update data. However, it is usually good practice to use the automatic checking offered by this mechanism, as it guarantees consistency, eases the work of the programmer, optimizes checking of referential integrity, and defends the database schema from programmer inconsistencies (a programmer can produce code that does not maintain this consistency manually). On the other hand, if referential integrity is enforced by means of foreign keys, the programmer is expected to provide any exception handling that might be necessary in case an attempted violation raises some exception (as with any other kind of handling of integrity constraints).

Most frequently, a foreign key is an attribute or set of attributes that is primary key in some other relation. This follows from the fact that primary keys are unique identifiers of tuples, and a foreign key most frequently references individual tuples of another relation.

2.6. Domain and Business Rule Constraints

We mentioned domain constraints before. Given an attribute, we define its data type, which identifies the predefined set to which it belongs. Some well-known mathematical sets are used as predefined domains in DBMS, including natural numbers (N), integer numbers (Z) and real numbers (R). Typical data types is DBMS are translations of these, plus other sets defined to ease the representation and operation over other types of data, such as strings, dates, datetime, timestamps and so on.

It is very important for the R-DBMS to provide as much built-in functionality as possible, so that the users declare what they need instead of having to code how to determine what they need. For that reasons R-DBMS provide not only most data types that may be needed, as they also provide operations (functions) to use with those data types. For instance, there are many pre-defined operations to handle dates and strings. Available string functions include functions to find a substring or similar strings; date functions include all sorts of operations, for instance a conversion between dates formatted as strings to dates, or computing how many months, days or hours there are between two dates.

Figure 10 and Figure 11 show examples of data types. The ones in Figure 10 are subsets of integer data types, while Figure 11 illustrates other data types. For all those data types, the DBMS includes a set of functions that help users manage the data types and compute what they need in their applications.

	Integer numbers	
Storage	Name	Range
Numeric 1 byte	tinyint(n)	-127 to 127
Numeric 2 bytes	smallint(n)	-32768 to 32768
...	...	...
Numeric 4 bytes	int(n)	+/-2.147E+9
Numeric 8 bytes	bigint(n)	+/-9.22E+18

Figure 10. Data Types: Integer Numbers

Examples of Other types	observations
numeric(n)	subset of integers
numeric(n,p) or decimal(n,p)	decimal number, with n digits and precision p, a subset of real
float(p)	decimal number, with precision p
char(n)	fixed size string
varchar(n)	variable size string
text	text upt o 65535 chars
longtext	text up to 4G chars
Blob	binary large object
long blob	long binary large object
date	
datetime	date and time
time	
timestamp	
year	

Figure 11. Data Types: Other types

The data type itself imposes a set of constraints in the data that could be represented using them. For instance, if we use a tinyint data type, we can only represent values from -127 to 127 (2^8 combinations of 8 bits). If we use a numeric data type with the formulation numeric(n,p), we can only represent up to n digits and with a precision of up to p decimal digits. If we choose data type varchar(n), the string can have only up to n characters. An attribute with type date cannot represent the day 31th of February.

To those constraints we can add additional constraints in the form of predicates. For instance, Algorithm 6 states that the value of most attribute cannot be NULL, by specifying NOT NULL in the table creation statement.

We can add any other constraint that we need to enforce. For instance, if the income should not be more than 20,000, then we add a predicate in the form of a check primitive to the table creation statement. In Algorithm 6 the date of birth cannot be less than 1900 and it cannot also be larger than the current date (now()). In the example the function todate in the predicate "function > todate('dd/mm/yy','01/01/1900')" allows the user to specify a date as a string with any format, as long as the format is included as the second argument to the call to function todate. In Algorithm 6 there is also a constraint predicate on income, stating that it should be positive or zero, and less than 20,000. In mathematical terms,

$$\text{Income} \in Z \text{ AND Income} >= 0 \text{ AND Income} < 20000$$

```
 CREATE TABLE Person(
IdentityCardID Numeric(12) PRIMARY KEY,
FirstName varchar(50) NOT NULL,
MiddleInitial varchar(50) NULL,
LastName varchar(50) NOT NULL,
Address varchar(100) NOT NULL,
City varchar(50) NOT NULL,
ZipCode varchar(10) NOT NULL,
Country String varchar(50) NOT NULL,
PhoneNumber varchar(14) NOT NULL,
DateOfBirth Date
CHECK(date > todate('dd/mm/yy','01/01/1900') and date < now()),
Income numeric(5) CHECK(income>=0 and income < 20000)
);
```
Algorithm 6. Example of Create table with explicit constraints

Business rules are any kind of rules related to the model of the organization that result in constraints over what values the attributes can take. The constraints defined in Algorithm 6 can be seen as business rules, but other more complex business rules can also be defined. For instance, nobody should have an income that is larger than the income of the boss, or the amount of stock of a product needs to be always larger than the monthly demand for that product, which varies along the year. Many business rules cannot be expressed as check statements, or it may be too impractical to do so. Defining constraints and business rules as check statements to be enforced by the R-DBMS is not compulsory, even the less complex constraints. What should be mandatory is for the designers to document carefully all constraints and business rules while they are designing, so that programmers will take those into account in the code. Complex business rules should be written down in a specification of the database to build, and programmers should make sure they include the business rules as constraints somehow, that the code checks those constraints and business rules, and that they handle exceptions arising from attempted violations of constraints.

2.7. Handling Violations of Integrity Constraints

An application should not stop working, return strange error messages to users or let the data become inconsistent. To avoid those problems, it is necessary to plan adequately what possible violations of constraints and business rules can happen and what should be done when those happen.

For instance, the user interface of a database application usually requires the programmer to validate input fields that are filled by users, and in those validations he is expected to check constraints on the admissible values for the input field.

Besides validating data, the programmer must take care of exceptions when the R-DBMS returns an exception due to violations of constraints. For instance, consider that a primary key was defined for a relation. The Mysql error code for duplicate data entry into the field that is a primary key is:

ERROR 1062 (23000): Duplicate entry 'xxxxxx' for key 'MyPrimaryKey'

In Java this can be handled using a try-catch block as shown next,

```
Try {
        // insert code here
}catch(SQLException se) {
      if(se.getErrorCode()==1062)
                // handle duplicate entry error here
                // e.g. indicate error to user
}
```

Algorithm 7. Try-catch example

2.8. Relational Algebra Operations and Extensions

Relational algebra operations take one (unary) or two (binary) relations as operands and return a relation as output. Relational algebra operations can be applied in sequence, since both operands and results are relations.

For binary operations, given relations R and S, and operation op_A, the result of (R op_A S) is still a relation. If T is another relation, the result of an operation B applied as (R op_A S) op_B T is still a relation.

Given a unary operation op_A, $op_A(R)$ is also a relation. Therefore, we can apply unary operations in sequence, such as in $op_B(op_A(R))$. Given relations R and S, unary operation op_A and binary operation op_B, S op_B ($op_A(R)$) is valid and is a relation. Likewise, the operation $op_A(R op_B S)$ is also valid and a relation.

The following operations of set theory are also defined in relational algebra, over relations:

Intersection ($\cap$) – the intersection of relations R and S (R $\cap$ S) is the set of elements (tuples) that are common to R and S;

Union ($\cup$) – the union of relations R and S (R $\cup$ S) is the set whose elements are those of R and S;

41

Set Difference (\) – the set difference of relations R and S (R\S) is the set whose elements are in R and not in S;

Cartesian Product (×) – the cartesian product of relations R and S (R×S) is the set of all ordered pairs (C,D) such that C∈R and D∈S.

Most importantly, relational algebra defines an additional set of operations and extensions that are very useful for the SQL relational query language, including:

Projection (π) – Projection is a unary operation that returns a relation with a subset of the attributes of the input relation. If the input relation is defined as R = { {tu$_i$ }, (a$_1$,..,a$_n$, a$_{n+1}$,..,a$_m$)}, where tu$_i$ are tuples and a$_i$ are the attributes defined for the relation, relation R = { {tu$_i$'}, (a$_1$,..,a$_n$)} is a projection of R, tu$_i$' are the same tuples as tu$_i$ without the values of attributes a$_{n+1}$,..,a$_m$ which were removed by the projection operation.

Example: the projection π (FirstName, MiddleInitial, LastName) over relation Patient(PatientID, FirstName, MiddleInitial, LastName, Address, City, ZipCode, Country, PhoneNumber, DateOfBirth) has the same number of tuples as the relation, but only the first, middle and last names of each patient.

In SQL, this projection would be written as,

SELECT FirstName, MiddleInitial, LastName FROM Person;

Selection (σ) - Selection is a unary operation that applies a predicate on attributes of the relation to select a subset of tuples (it is written as $\sigma_{predicate}$). The predicate, when applied to each tuple of the relation individually, evaluates to true or false. The output of the selection operator is the relation with a subset of the tuples from the initial relation that evaluate to true for the predicate.

Example: the selection $\sigma_{lastname='Gomes'}$Person retrieves all tuples of relation 'Person' with last name 'Gomes'. The result is a relation ($\sigma_{lastname='Gomes'}$Person) having all persons with last name 'Gomes'.

This selection would be written in SQL as,

SELECT * FROM Person where lastName='Gomes';

Join (inner join) (∞) – join is a binary operation that takes two relations (R and S) as input, and returns a relation R∞S that matches tuples from both relations for which a join predicate evaluates to true. The join predicate is most often a predicate testing whether the value of the join attribute(s) of one relation match the value of the join attribute(s) of the other relation.

Example: the join

$$(\text{Patient } \infty_{\text{Patient.patientID=MedicalProcedure.patient}} \text{ MedicalProcedure})$$

outputs every combination of tuples form Patient and MedicalProcedure that match. This join would be written in SQL as,

SELECT Patient.*, MedicalProcedure.*
FROM Patient JOIN MedicalProcedure
ON Patient.patientID = MedicalProcedure.patient;

Another syntax expresses the join as a selection predicate on both relations,

SELECT Patient.*, MedicalProcedure.*
FROM Patient, MedicalProcedure
WHERE Patient.patientID = MedicalProcedure.patient;

There are also some variants of the join operation. First of all, the previous example is an equi-join (a join based on the equality of a pair of attributes from the relations). In some (rare) cases, the join condition is not an equality, for instance a join between Person and TaxedBy(salaryLow, salaryHigh, tax) determine the tax based on the salary:

SELECT Person.lastName, TaxedBy.tax
FROM Person, TaxedBy
WHERE Person.salary > TaxedBy.salaryLow and
Person.salary < TaxedBy.salaryLow;

Outer join (full outer join) – the outer join extends the results returned by the inner join. It also includes unmatched tuples from the two relations in the output relation. Attributes of the relation with whom there was no match for a specific tuple are filled NULL in the output tuple.

Left join and **Right join** – Similar to full outer join, but only includes non-matching tuples from one of the relations, the left or right relations respectively.

SELECT Patient.*, MedicalProcedure.*
FULL OUTER JOIN Patient, MedicalProcedure
ON Patient.patientID = MedicalProcedure.patient;

SELECT Patient.*, MedicalProcedure.*
LEFT JOIN Patient, MedicalProcedure
ON Patient.patientID = MedicalProcedure.patient;

SELECT Patient.*, MedicalProcedure.*
RIGHT JOIN Patient, MedicalProcedure
ON Patient.patientID = MedicalProcedure.patient;

Aggregation $(G_1...G_n \ g \ f_1(A_1).. \ f_p(A_m) \ (R) \ )$ – Consider a relation R, attributes (or expressions on attributes) $G_1,...,G_n$ of R, and functions $f_1(A_1)...f_p(A_m)$, where:

1. $G_1,...,G_n$ are attributes (or expressions on attributes) of R denoted as the "group-by attributes";

2. A_1 to A_m are attributes (or expressions on attributes) of R denoted as "aggregation attributes";

3. $f_i()$ are functions that operate on attributes or expressions on attributes. The attributes or expressions are used to compute a set of values $\{v1,...,v_n\}$ over a relation, and the function returns a value f_i for the set of values;

4. f_i is denoted as "summary" or "aggregation" of the values.

The aggregation g is an operation that computes summaries $f_1,...,f_x$ for each subset of R that is determined by selecting the tuples of R that match each possible combination of values of the "group-by attributes". The sets of values over which the summaries $f_1,...,f_x$ are computed are those obtained by projecting/computing the expressions on "aggregation attributes" for each of the tuples of each subset.

Although the definition of aggregation is somewhat complex, it is a very powerful operator that can be applied to understand the characteristics of data very easily. For instance, if we have a Sales dataset, which records the sales along time, we can compute sales evolution according to any time granularity (e.g. day, week, month, year). If the dataset contains attributes "salesVolume" and "salesDate")(i.e. it is the relation Sales(salesVolume, salesDate,...), we can obtain monthly sales by issuing the following SQL query,

SELECT sum(salesVolume) as Sales,
             to_char(salesDate,'mm-yyyy') as MonthYear
FROM sales
GROUP BY to_char(salesDate,'mm-yyyy');

Figure 12 shows the relation, the output of the query and the same output as a sales chart. If we wanted to know the evolution of sales per week, we would only have to replace the expression to_char(salesDate,'mm-yyyy') by to_char(salesDate,'week-yyyy'), and if we want to restrict the values shown to a single year, we only have to add a where clause (selection), such as "where to_char(salesDate,'yyyy')='2014',

SELECT   sum(salesVolume) as Sales,
             to_char(salesDate,'mm-yyyy') as MonthYear
FROM sales
WHERE to_char(salesDate,'yyyy')='2014'
GROUP BY to_char(salesDate,'mm-yyyy');

Pedro Furtado

salesVolume	salesDate
1000	1/1/14
876	1/2/14
976	1/3/14
765	1/4/14
453	1/5/14
1098	1/6/14
...	...

Sales	MonthYear
30000	01-2014
26280	02-2014
29280	03-2014
22950	04-2014
...	...
18360	10-2014
10872	11-2014
26352	12-2014
...	...

(a) The Sales Relation   (b) Query Output

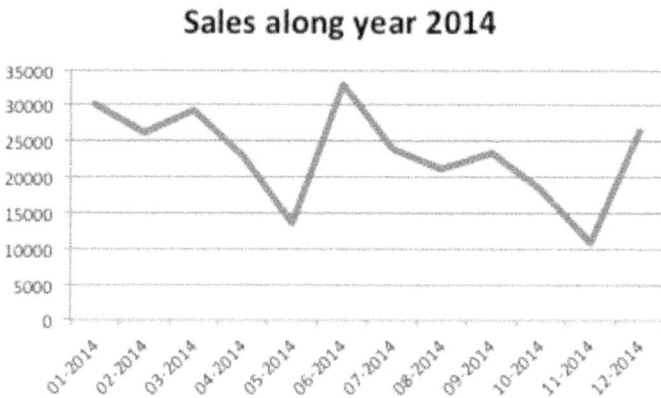

(c) Query Output as a Sales Chart

Figure 12. Sales Relation and Query Output

The previous example shows how powerful aggregation can be. There are many other aggregation functions that can be applied to obtain different types of aggregations over datasets. These include the count (number of elements), sum, average, standard deviation, percentiles, minimum, maximum.

3. Structured Query Lang. (SQL)

We already used some SQL constructs as we introduced the relational model and associated concepts in the previous chapter. In this chapter we describe SQL in more detail, and the next chapter contains exercises that will allow the reader to train using SQL. We do not cover SQL exhaustively, instead we focus on guiding the user to understand the most important concepts and to start his autonomous exploration of the subject. Readers already familiar with SQL can skip this chapter. Additional bibliography on SQL includes [10] and [11].

3.1. SQL as a Programming Language

The first issue that should be discussed regarding SQL is where it stands as a programming language. Some students do not like SQL, when they learn about it for the first time. One typical argument is that it looks like a low-level or archaic language. Java or Python seem a lot more modern and advanced than SQL.

SQL is a declarative language, which sets it apart from most usual programming languages. Different programming languages have been created along time that followed one or another paradigm. Examples of very disparate programming language paradigms are logic programming (e.g. Prolog), list-based programming (Lisp), mathematical programming tools (e.g. Matlab), procedural languages (C, C++, Java, Python, most other programming languages), object-oriented languages (C++, Java, Python), imperative and declarative languages. SQL is a declarative language based on the relational model and algebra.

Some of the most competent, popular and commonly used languages are object-oriented and procedural. Some typical procedural primitives (e.g. cycles, conditional statements) give programmers flexibility to specify the steps to accomplish some task, and object orientation allows programmers to abstract behaviors and state into objects with well-defined interfaces and behaviors.

By contrast to procedural thinking, in a declarative language users are expected to specify what they want instead of the steps that are necessary to get what they want. This is a clear superiority of declarative languages that places them higher in terms of abstraction than classic procedural languages. For instance, in SQL we specify that we want to retrieve the full name and address of anyone whose last name starts by the character 'S',

```
SELECT lastName, firstName, address
FROM Person
WHERE lastName like 'S%';
```

With only this command we are given an output relation (table) with the desired results. In order to do the same using procedural thinking, we should open a file for reading, create a cycle that reads it row-by-row, parse each row into an in-memory 'Person' record, test if the last name field of that record starts by 'S'. If it starts by 'S', then create a new record with (fullName, address) fields, add the values to the newly created record and add that record to an array of records containing output records. Object Orientation can help encapsulate this behavior into objects and re-use the code, but it still looks like a lower-level of abstraction than declarative languages. Declarative languages eliminate most of the trouble of instructing the system how to do the operations. The details of how to do the operations are left to the implementation of the language or system that processes the language commands.

Of course, if this was the whole story, declarative languages would always be preferable when compared with procedural or object-oriented languages. Such is not the case. First of all, high levels of abstraction are possible using modularization and object orientation. These allow the details of functionality to be hidden from users who reuse, instead of implementing all the details. And while declarative languages restrict what can be done by what the model is able to represent and how it is able to operate, procedural/object oriented languages provide a high degree of flexibility in what can be implemented. That is why declarative and mathematical languages are usually also complemented by procedural/object oriented capabilities. Declarative and higher-level models ease the job of programmers when using the core functionality for which the languages were developed, while object orientation and procedural capabilities allow programmers to further extend the capabilities and to have more flexibility. The declarative or mathematical models themselves are frequently abstractions that were created in some procedural object-oriented language to create a higher-level of abstraction for the core functionalities that are reused.

SQL is also a standard. The standard created a common base language instead of each database engine having its own syntax and operational models. This effort was quite successful, since today we can program in SQL and adapt that program to any specific relational database engine that we may want to use (some modifications are usually still necessary, since different engines have their own particularities, but it is easy to port SQL between database engines).

Besides SQL, many database engines also provide an associated procedural language. For instance, Oracle provides PL/SQL (PL stands for procedural language), and PostgresSQL™ provides pgSQL. The reason for those extensions is to provide the advantages of declarative models together with the flexibility of procedural programming.

3.2. Servers, Clients and SQL

In order to use SQL, client applications need to connect to a database server. A database server is a database management system (DBMS) installed in a server machine and that includes a "service" that listens for client connections (usually through a TCP port). When a connection is established, after some handshake and user authentication, the client application can submit requests in the form of SLQ statements. The server DBMS contains all the executable code that parses, interprets and runs the routines to answer the SQL statements. When the request arrives, it is executed and the server returns the results to the client application. All most used DBMS come with one or more client applications that may be web-based or not (console) for submitting SQL commands. We call this application an SQL client. In order to experiment with SQL, or to build and test schemas and queries, you need to install the DBMS and then call the SQL client.

3.3. Data Definition Language (SQL-DDL)

The Data Definition Language (DDL) is a set of SQL commands necessary to define, modify or delete relations and auxiliary structures. It allows users to create, modify and delete relations (tables), views, indexes and other objects.

We already saw examples of CREATE TABLE commands. Algorithm 8 shows the template of the command and an example.

We also discussed the elements that are used to define data types, sizes and integrity constraints. The following are typical constraints and parameters:

NULL/NOT NULL – constraint specifying that the attribute can or cannot take null values;

UNIQUE – constraint specifying that the attribute cannot have duplicate values (all values taken by this attribute in the relation must be unique);

```
CREATE TABLE <RelationName>
(ColumnName    DataType(size|precision) Integrity Constraints,
…);
```

(a) CREATE TABLE Template

```
CREATE TABLE Person(
IdentityCardID Numeric(12) PRIMARY KEY,
FirstName varchar(50) NOT NULL,
MiddleInitial varchar(50) NULL,
LastName varchar(50) NOT NULL,
Address varchar(100) NOT NULL,
City varchar(50)   NOT NULL,
ZipCode varchar(10) NOT NULL,
Country String varchar(50) NOT NULL,
PhoneNumber varchar(14) NOT NULL,
Employer Numeric(12)
          Constraint employerNotNull NOT NULL,
DateOfBirth Date
          CHECK(DateOfBirth > todate('dd/mm/yy','01/01/1900')
          and DateOfBirth < now()),
Income numeric(5)
          CHECK(income>=0 and income < 20000),
FOREIGN KEY employer REFERENCES Employer(employerID)
);
```

(b) CREATE TABLE Example

Algorithm 8. Example of CREATE TABLE statement

PRIMARY KEY – identifies the column as a primary key, adding a primary key constraint. A primary key is also unique and non null, therefore those two constraints are pre-defined for a primary key;

FOREIGN KEY – creates a referential integrity constraint. It identifies an attribute from the relation (the foreign key) and indicates that it references another attribute from another relation (the referenced attribute of the foreign key). In the example of Algorithm 8, the attribute Employer references attribute employerID of relation Employer;

CHECK – allows users to add constraints in the form of predicates that must evaluate to true for the attribute value to be valid (does not allow addition of an attribute value that does not evaluate to true under the predicate). In the example of Algorithm 8, the income specified in an insert command must be between 0 and 20,000 for the command to be successful, an exception is raised otherwise;

CONSTRAINT constraintName - specifies the name of the constraint. Any constraint can be given a name. The name "employerNotNull" is an example in Algorithm 8;

Relations can also be created from other relations, based on some query,

CREATE TABLE <RelationName>
(ColumnName 1,…, ColumnName n)
AS SQLquery ;
       (a)   CREATE TABLE from Query - Template

CREATE TABLE PersonFromCoimbra
AS SELECT IdentityCardID, FirstName, LastName
FROM Person
WHERE City='Coimbra';
      (b) CREATE TABLE from Query - Example

Algorithm 9. CREATE TABLE from Query

A VIEW is a "virtual relation" that is specified using a query over a relation. For that reason, a VIEW always has an associated query that defines it. For instance, the previous relation PersonFromCoimbra could be replaced by a view shown in Algorithm 10. The difference between this and the previous alternative is that the data is not stored in a new relation, instead only the text of the query is kept for use when the view is used as a source relation in a query.

We can use either the view created in Algorithm 10 or the relation created in Algorithm 9 in the query of Algorithm 11,

```
CREATE VIEW PersonFromCoimbra
AS
SELECT IdentityCardID, FirstName, LastName
FROM Person
WHERE City='Coimbra';
```
Algorithm 10. CREATE VIEW command


```
SELECT LastName
FROM PersonFromCoimbra
Where FistName like 'S%';
```
Algorithm 11. Query over VIEW or RELATION

The CREATE command is associated with the creation of any object in the database. For instance, an index is an auxiliary structure made to speedup access to specific tuples of the database, by providing an ordered search. For instance, if we have a big relation Person and we want to find a person named 'Gil Quadros', if there is an index on field lastName, the DBMS might answer the query faster by searching through the index (the DBMS decides automatically if it uses the index, depending on its estimation of the cost of processing the query with or without the index). If we want to create an index on lastName, we simply issue the command,

CREATE INDEX lastName ON Person(lastName);

The opposite to CREATE is a DROP, which deletes (drops) the object from the database. In order to drop relation Person, we need to specify the command DROP TABLE PERSON;

If we want to modify the structure of an object in the database, we can use ALTER commands. We can add or remove attributes, modify an attribute, add or remove constraints to relations, as long as we do not violate the constraints on data that the relation may already have. Algorithm 12 shows the template of the alter table command, and examples.

```
ALTER TABLE <RelationName>
ADD(attributeName attribute definition) |
ADD CONSTRAINT (constraint definition) |
MODIFY (attributeName new attribute definition) |
DROP CONSTRAINT (constraintName);
```
                (a) ALTER TABLE (Template)

```
ALTER TABLE Person
        ADD employer Numeric(12),
        ADD CONSTRAINT employer NOT NULL,
        MODIFY CONSTRAINT firstName NULL,
        DROP middleName;
```
                (b) ALTER TABLE Example

Algorithm 12. ALTER TABLE command

3.4. Data Manipulation Language (SQL-DML)

The data manipulation language consists of commands that modify the contents of relations. They include insert, update and delete commands. Algorithm 13 shows the template of the insert command and an example, inserting patients into the Patient relation that was defined in Figure 2.

```
INSER INTO <RelationName> [attributeName 1,...,attributeName n]
VALUES(value 1, ..., value n);
```
                (a) INSERT command (Template)

```
INSERT INTO Patient
VALUES(19845, 'Joaquim', 'N.', 'Gomes', 'Rua Castilho, 23',
'Lisboa', '2720-234','Portugal', '91-99893','2/10/2000');
```
                (b) INSERT command Example

Algorithm 13.INSERT INTO TABLE command

It is possible to insert multiple tuples in the same command by specifying multiple values clauses separated by commas (without repeating the VALUES keyword).

INSERT INTO Patient VALUES
(19845, 'Joaquim', 'N.', 'Gomes', 'Rua Castilho, 23', 'Lisboa',
'2720-234', 'Portugal', '91-99893', '2/10/2000'),
(19846, 'Joao', 'M.', 'Silva', 'Rua Malmequer, 2', 'Porto',
'2154-244', 'Portugal', '91-59873', '1/1/2003');
Algorithm 14. INSERT MULTIPLE command

Also very useful is the command to insert values into a relation by specifying a query that retrieves values from other relation(s) to insert into the other one. Algorithm 15 shows insertion of persons from Coimbra in a table with that name by retrieving all persons from Coimbra from the Person table and inserting those in the PersonFromCoimbra table.

INSERT INTO PersonFromCoimbra
        SELECT IdentityCardID, FirstName, LastName
FROM Person
WHERE City='Coimbra';
Algorithm 15. INSERT SELECT command

The "INSERT SELECT" command of Algorithm 15 requires relation PersonFromCoimbra to be created before, while the command Algorithm 9 creates the table from scratch directly using the query.

The "opposite command" of INSERT is "DELETE". Its template is shown in Algorithm 16, while Algorithm 17 shows an example that deletes all persons with last name starting by 'S'. The WHERE clause specifies a predicate that is applied to filter the tuples that should be deleted. For each tuple, if the predicate evaluates to true, then the tuple is removed from the relation.

DELETE FROM RelationName
    WHERE <condition>
    Algorithm 16. DELETE command template

DELETE FROM PersonFromCoimbra
    WHERE lastName like 'S%';
    Algorithm 17. DELETE command example

The last DML command that we review is the UPDATE command. Algorithm 18 shows the template of the command, and the example of Algorithm 19 applies the template. In that command all persons with last name starting by 'S' are assigned Lisboa and Portugal as city and country respectively.

UPDATE <relationName>
    SET   attribute 1=assignment expression 1,
          attribute 2= assignment expression 2,
          …,
          attribute n=assignment expression n
    [WHERE condition];
Algorithm 18. UPDATE command template
UPDATE PersonFromCoimbra
    SET   City='Lisboa',
          Country='Portugal'
WHERE lastName like 'S%';
    Algorithm 19. UPDATE command example

3.5. Query Language (SQL-QL) and Query Clauses

The SQL query language (SQL-QL) consists of statements expressed using SELECT statements. SELECT statements are the main construct used to submit queries that retrieve and process data. Such statements follow the model of relational operations (relational algebra). An SQL query can also be seen conceptually as a composition of relational operations. The input operand(s) and the output operand of each relational operation are relations themselves, and the output can serve as input to the next operation. SQL statements can also be nested themselves using sub-queries. Since a sub-query is an SQL statement, the output is a relation, which can be an input to an outer query.

If we look at the execution of an SQL query as a sequence of relational operations, each step of the sequence is a relational operation whose input(s) is/are relations and whose output is a relation. Since there are usually a set of steps in the sequence, the output of a step that is simultaneously an input of the next step is called an intermediate result.

The following are two examples of SQL queries. The first query does not aggregate, while the second query is an aggregation query,

Q1:
SELECT Patient.LastName, medP.Symptoms, medP.procDate,
FROM Patient, MedicalProcedure medP
WHERE Patient.patientID = MedicalProcedure.patient
AND Patient.LastName='Silva';
ORDER BY medP.procDate desc;

Q1 retrieves all symptoms of patient 'Silva' (in fact, of every patient whose last name is Silva), ordered by the date of the medical procedure. This query does a JOIN between two relations, applies a SELECTION predicate to constrain to 'Silva', PROJECTs a set of output attributes (LastName, Symptoms, Procedure date), and ORDERs the data output tuples based on the date of the procedure.

Q2:
SELECT Patient.LastName, Patient.FirstName,
            count(*) as NumMedProcedures
FROM Patient, MedicalProcedure
WHERE Patient.patientID = MedicalProcedure.patient
GROUP BY Patient.LastName, Patient.FirstName;

Q2 counts the number of medical procedures that each patient has undergone. In order to do that, it needs to JOIN relations Patient and

MedicalProcedure and to apply an aggregation operation, grouping by attributes LastName and FirstName and using, as aggregation function, a count to count the number of occurrences of each specific group (a group is identified by the pair LastName, FirstName) in the intermediate dataset.

An SQL query is made of a set of clauses, as indicated in Algorithm 20. Queries can have subsets of those clauses, but the SELECT and FROM clauses always need to be present.

SELECT selectExpressions
FROM relation(s)
(JOIN relation ON joinPredicate)
WHERE constraintsExpression
GROUP BY groupByAttributes
HAVING expressionsOnGroupByAttrs
ORDER BY orderingExpression
Algorithm 20. SQL-QL Statement Clauses

Next we describe each clause:

SELECT selectExpressions – this clause specifies a set of attributes or expressions operating on attributes of the relations involved in the query. These attributes or expressions determine the values that are output by the query. The select expressions are applied to each row after it is retrieved and operated according to other query clauses. The simplest expression might be a constant (C), or an attribute of a relation referenced in the FROM clause. Expressions can involve function calls and arithmetic operations on attributes. For instance, to_char(birthdate, 'dd-mm-yy') outputs the value of attribute birthdate using a specific formating. If a and b are numeric attributes, SELECT $a+b$ will output the sum of the values of those attributes for each row of the dataset(s) involved in the query.

In terms of relational operators, the SELECT clause is usually said to implement the operator 'projection', since it projects (restricts) the attributes of the relation that are to be included in the output relation. In practice, the use of expressions, functions and all sorts of operations in the SELECT clause extends the projection operator;

FROM relations – the FROM clause indicates which relations will be sources for the query. If a query specifies relations A and B as sources, the data that will be operated upon will be from those relations;

(JOIN relation ON joinPredicate) – the JOIN clause specifies which relations join to which other relations (this is the join operator of relational algebra) and based on which join predicates. Any two tuples from the two joined datasets are output in a join iff the join predicate evaluates to true.

Instead of using the syntax JOIN...ON, it is more usual to list all relations that are to be joined in the FROM clause, and to specify the join predicates in the WHERE clause, together with other selection predicates.

The following examples help clarify the concept of a join. Consider relations R(j,a) and S(l,b,j), where a,b,j,l are attributes. Attribute j is a primary key in R, referenced by foreign key j of S. Algorithm 21(a) shows the query that should be submitted to output tuples formed with pairs (R.a, S.b). The WHERE clause includes the join predicate R.j=S.j that matches rows with matching values of attribute j.

Consider a third relation T(c,m), where m is an attribute in T that references l, the primary key of S. Algorithm 21 shows the query that should be submitted, and in particular which join predicates need to be included, to output triples (R.a, S.b, T.c), by joining the three relations using the attributes that make the link between the relations R, S and T.

Select R.a, S.b	Select R.a, S.b, T.c
From R, S	From R, S, T
Where R.j=S.j	Where R.j=S.j and S.l=T.m

(a) Joining two relations	(b) Joining three relations

Algorithm 21. Queries joining two and three relations

One simple rule of thumb is that, if the FROM clause lists n relations, there should be a conjunction of $n-1$ join predicates on the primary keys. In Algorithm 21(a) there are two relations and one join predicate, while in (b) there are three relations and two join predicates.

To apply the rule of thumb correctly when the join attributes between two relations are based in more than one attribute, we must keep in mind that the join predicate in that case is itself a conjunction. For instance, given relations $R(j_1,j_2,a)$ and $S(l,b,j_1,j_2)$, where j_1,j_2 are primary keys in R and a foreign key in S referencing R, there is a single join predicate with two conditions, the one shown in Algorithm 22.

Select R.a, S.b
From R, S
Where $R.j_1=S.j_1$ and $R.j_2=S.j_2$

Algorithm 22. Joining two relations on two attributes

Whenever we are joining relations, the join predicates need to be included, otherwise a Cartesian product (x) of the relations will happen. Given relations R with size r and S with size s (size meaning the number of tuples), relation RxS will have size (r x s), since every tuple of r will be matched with every tuple of s. That is not what you usually want in a join, since you usually want to find matches between a primary key in one of the relations (e.g. R) and a foreign key referencing it in the other relation (e.g. S). The output of the join between R and S should have the size of S, since each tuple of S will be matched by a tuple of R.

WHERE constraints – the WHERE clause corresponds to the relational algebra operator "selection". The "constraints" part is a predicate, frequently made of sets of predicates linked by conjunctions and disjunctions. The "constraints" predicate is applied to each tuple of the relation(s) to determine whether it will be filtered in or out of the intermediate result that is output at this step (if the predicate evaluates to true or false, respectively).

In the example of Algorithm 23 all tuples are retrieved from the relation Person and the predicate "lastName Like 'Silva%' and birthdate>1970" is applied to each tuple. If the predicate evaluates to true, the tuple is output to the next operation of the query. In the case of this query, the next operation is the projection of the last name of the person. Consequently, the output of the query is all last names of all persons with lastname like Silva% (Silva followed by any characters) and birthdate after 1970.

SELECT lastName
FROM Person
WHERE lastName Like 'Silva%' and birthdate>1970

Algorithm 23. Where clause: illustrative example

GROUP BY groupByAttributes – the GROUP BY clause, together with selectExpressions that specify aggregation functions, specify an aggregation operation, as we defined in the previous section when we described aggregation as an operation of the relational model.

Given our previous definition of the aggregation operator ($G_1...G_n$ g $f_1(A_1).. f_p(A_m)$ (R)), the group-by attributes $G_1...G_n$ are those specified in the clause 'GROUP BY groupByAttrs', and the aggregation functions $f_1().. f_p()$ are those specified in the select clause 'SELECT selectExpressions'. The last clause, 'HAVING expressionsOnGroupByAttributes' specifies a selection predicate expression on the groups that are obtained by the aggregation.

Algorithm 24 shows an example. The average salary of each job is computed for all jobs with average salary above 200,000.

SELECT average(salary), job
FROM Consultant
GROUP BY job
HAVING average(salary)>200,000;

Algorithm 24. Aggregation: illustrative example

ORDER BY – the objective of the ORDER BY clause is to create a sort order of the output relation for presentation purposes, based on the specification of ordering attributes. The order of presentation is defined by a sorting of the tuples based on the ordering attributes (or expressions) specified in the ORDER BY clause. The tuples will be sorted according to the sorting order of the first attribute appearing in the clause, then, for tuples with same value of that attribute, according to the second attribute and so on. The ordering function depends on the data type (e.g. numeric, alphabetical or date ordering), and we can also specify ascending (keyword asc, the default ordering) or descending order (desc).

3.6. An Illustration of Query Operations Sequence

Figure 13 illustrates the conceptual operations of a Select-where query, assuming no join for simplicity. An initial relation is scanned (FROM relation); each tuple being retrieved is filtered using the selection predicate (constraints in WHERE constraints), determining the subset of tuples that proceed; the projection expressions (in SELECT selectExpressions) will retrieve a subset of columns from those tuples and apply operators and functions. Finally, ORDER BY attributes will be used to sort output tuples into a final order.

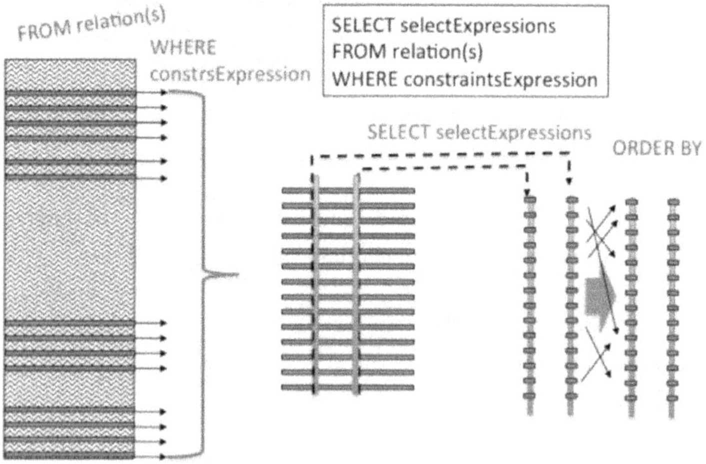

Figure 13. Illustrating Operations of Select-where Query

Figure 14 illustrates the conceptual operations of an Aggregation query, assuming no join, for simplicity. As in the Select-where case, an initial relation is scanned (FROM relation); each tuple being retrieved is filtered using the constraint expressions (WHERE constrsExpression), determining the subset of tuples that proceed. The GROUP BY clause organizes the tuples into groups according to the values of the GROUP BY attributes (G1,...,Gn), and computes aggregation functions specified in the SELECT clause for each of those groups. The last clause HAVING applies a predicate on the groups, to restrict those that are kept in the final result.

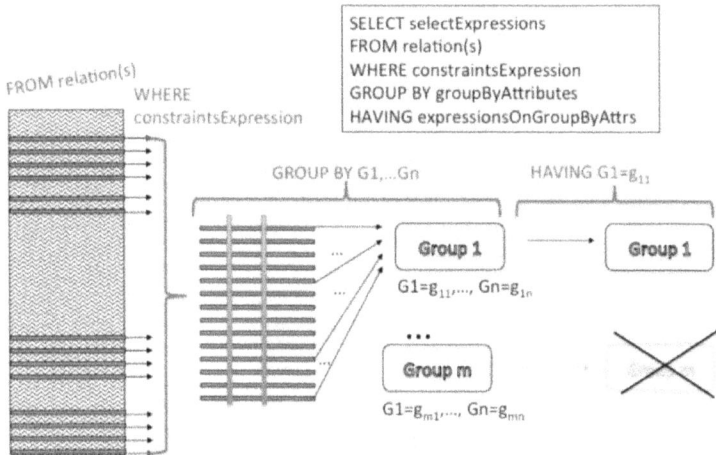

Figure 14. Illustrating Operations of Aggregation Query

Figure 15 illustrates the operation of a JOIN, followed by a selection based on a predicate. In order to make the join more explicit, we used the JOIN...ON clause. In the figure, relations R1 and R2 are scanned and, for each pair of tuples from both relations for which R1.a=R2.b (attributes a of R1 and b of R2 have the same value), there is a match. The tuple that results from concatenating those two tuples will be part of the output from this operation, to be processed further in the query.

The conceptual operations illustrated in Figure 13, Figure 14 and Figure

15 may not be the physical execution plans of the queries, because database engines optimize the order in which they apply relational operators, and might use different strategies and indexes to reduce the time needed to process a query. The discussion of how the RDBMS engine plans and optimizes its execution is out of the scope of this book.

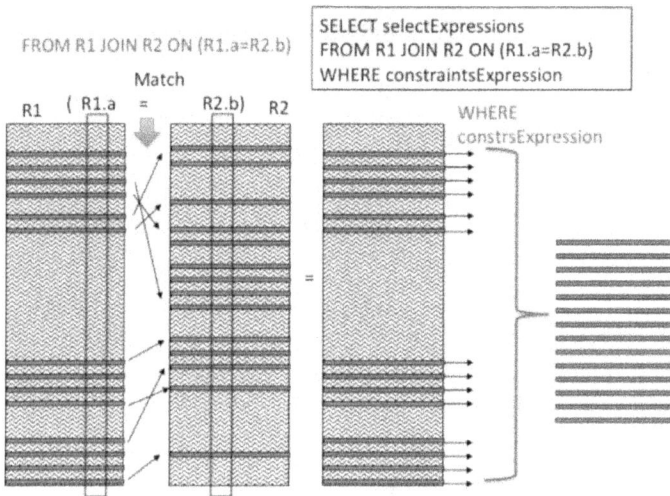

Figure 15. Illustrating Operations of Join

4. SQL Functions and Exercises

In this chapter we introduce a simple relational schema, present some commonly used functions and propose a set of exercises to experiment with some of the most interesting features of SQL. Examples are shown independently of the RDBMS where they would run, although small details may need to be changed to run on a specific platform.

4.1. Dummy Schema

The relational model that we will use is a dummy database of Tasks and Consultants doing the Tasks. The schema of the database is already given. In a later chapter we will show how to reason to arrive at an adequate representation of the schema.

Consider the schema shown in Algorithm 25. It represents Tasks of a Project identified by the number of the Task (taskNum) in the Project (projectID). The relation Project has a project ID (projectID) and a project name (projectName). The relation Task has fields 'title', 'description', 'needs', 'observations' and taskManager, which is someone assigned the responsibility for overseeing the Task. It also has fields identifying start and end dates of the project, both planned and actual. Then it includes estimation (planned) and actual (reported) needs of human resources, measured in Man-Months units (1 MM = one man working full time for a month, or two men working half time for a month). Finally, the Task also includes information on the budget (planned and reported). The primary key of Task (underlined) is (projectID, taskNum).

Task(projectID, taskNum,
title, description, needs, observations, taskManager,
startDateplanned, startDate, endDateplanned, endDate,
MMplanned, MMreported,
budgetplanned, budgetreported)

Project(projectID, projectName);

Algorithm 25. Project Database: Task and Project Entity

Consider also relation Consultant in Algorithm 26. Consultants supply the human resources that are necessary for the Tasks (Man-Months). The attributes associated with the Consultant are self-explanatory, except for ConsultantID, which is an identifier, either an artificial key or the identity card number. The supervisorID is the consultantID of the person who supervises the consultant, if he is a junior consultant, or none, if the consultant has no supervisor. Attribute taskManager in the task relation is a foreign key referencing the ID of a consultant, specifically the consultant who leads the task.

Consultant(consultantID, lastName, firstName, address, contacts,
supervisorID,
Job, expertise, curriculum,
hourlyRate, commission,
startDate, leaveDate)

Algorithm 26. Project Database: Entity Consultant

Finally, consider relation TaskConsultant in Algorithm 27, which represents the relationship between the two other entities. This relation identifies the project, the task number, the consultant (using consultantID), when he started working in the task, how many days he worked in the task, and a description of his job in the task.

TaskConsultant(projectID, taskNum, consultantID,
                       startDate, numberOfDays, description)
Algorithm 27. Project Database: TaskConsultant Entity

4.2. Tuple Functions and Operators

Tuple functions are functions that apply to each tuple that is retrieved. R-DBMS provide many such functions to fulfill operation needs. Since SQL is declarative by nature, it is important to provide as much functionality embedded as function calls as possible to allow users to express what they need using SQL statements.

There are also operators, which are invoked using operator symbols over one or two operands. Some of the most obvious operations are arithmetic, such as the sum (a+b), difference (a-b), division (a/b), multiplication (a*b) and the modulus (a % b), which are applicable to numeric attributes. Other pre-defined operations over non-numeric data types include the sum or difference between two dates (date 1 + date 2 or date 1 – date 2), or the concatenation of two strings (string 1 || string 2).

Expressions are constructs that can be used in most SQL clauses (selectExpressions, constraintsExpressions, groupByExpressions, havingExpressions, orderingExpressions). Expressions can be just attributes, but they can also be operations or function calls on expressions themselves (recursive definition of expression). The simplest expression is just a constant or an attribute, but much more complex expressions are built using operations and functions.

The list of functions is very extensive and varies according to the R-

DBMS that is being used. The best way to explore them is to search the web or SQL function references for the function that applies when something in concrete is needed. We will only list a few functions next as examples, and propose a few exercises to experiment with some of them. If a specific function does not run on a R-DBMS of your choice, search for a substitute in the web that applies to that R-DBMS.

The next examples apply a concatenation operator (||) to show how operators (or functions) can be applied in the context of the select clause of a query.

SELECT 'Hello ' || 'world' -> should output 'Hello world';

SELECT 'Hello ' || 'world' FROM task -> should output as many repetitions of 'Hello world' as there are tuples in relation Task. This is because it applies the operation to each tuple that is retrieved;

SELECT title || ':' || description FROM task -> should output a concatenation of the title with ':' and then with the description of the task, for each task.

4.2.1. String Functions

The syntax of SQL is not case sensitive, but operations with attributes of type string are case sensitive. The commands "select * from task" and "SELECT * FROM TASK" are the same, but "select * from task where title='Setup Information System' " is different from the command "select * from task where title='setup information system' ".

The following are some commonly used String functions:

CONCAT(String 1, String 2) and operator || (String 1 || String 2)- operates on two strings and outputs a concatenated string that is the result of continuing String 1 with String 2;

SUBSTR(String 1, pos [, n]) – returns a substring of String 1, starting in position pos and ending either at the end or n characters later;

INITCAP(String 1) – replaces the first character by an upper case character;

LPAD(String 1, n[, 'padString']), RPAD(String 1, n[, 'padString']) – adds white spaces or padString repetitions to the left (LPAD) or to the right (RPAD), until a total size of 'n' is reached;

LTRIM(String 1), RTRIM(String 1) – removes all whitespaces to the left or to the right of String 1;

REPLACE(String 1, StringOriginal, StringFinal) – replaces all occurrences of StringOriginal by StringFinal in String 1;

4.2.2. Examples of Date Functions

There is an extensive list of date functions that includes the following ones:

TO_CHAR(date [,'fmt']) – Converts a date into a string with the format indicated by the 'fmt' string. For instance, to_char(now(),'yyyy-mm-dd') returns today in the format of year (with four digits), month (two digits) and day in month (two digits as well), such as in '2025-11-23'.

TO_DATE(DateAsString [,'fmt']) – converts a date given as a string into a date object.

If we want to insert a new tuple in a relation R and one attribute is a date, we can issue an insert statement in which we convert a string to a date with the intended day in whichever format we want it to be in:

Insert into R values(..., to_date('2025-11-23','yyyy-mm-dd'),...);

ADD_MONTHS(date, n) or 'date + n months' – adds n months to the date;

(similar functions and operands exist for weeks and days);

MONTHS_BETWEEN(date 1, date 2) – returns the number of months between date 1 and date 2;

4.2.3. Examples of Arithmetic Functions

You can find almost any arithmetic function that you may need in the list of SQL functions of popular R-DBMS. Here are a few:

ABS(number) – returns the absolute value of number;

CEIL(number), FLOOR(number) – returns the lowest integer above the number or the highest integer below the number, respectively;

MOD(number1, number2) – same as number1 % number2, returns the modulo of number1 by number2;

POWER(number1, n) – returns the power of n of number1;

ROUND(number1, n) – returns the nearest integer to number1;

SQRT(number1) – returns the square root of the number;

4.2.4. Exercises

Exercise 1.
Show the first name, last name and job of every consultant. The first name should have the first letter only in caps, the last name should be all in caps, the job should be in lower case.

The result should be shown as (FirstName, LastName, Job).

Answer 1.
Select   initcap(lower(firstName)) as FirstName,
            upper(lastName) as LastName,
            lower(job) as Job
From Consultant;

Exercise 2.
Show the last name and hourly rate of consultants with an increase of 17.7% in their hourly rate. Round the resulting rate to the first decimal place.

Show the result as (lastName, New Hourly Rate).

Answer 2.

Select   lastName,

                round(1.177 * hourlyRate, 1) as "New Hourly Rate"

From Consultant;

4.3. Select, Project, Where and Order By

Exercise 1.

Compose a command to show all tasks whose title is 'Setup Information System', but the title may be written with upper or lower letters (case-insensitive).

What to do: you can use functions LOWER(attribute) or UPPER(attribute)).

Answer 1:

Select *

From task

Where lower(title)='setup information system';

Exercise 2.

Show the names and addresses of consultants (firstName, lastName, address) whose address starts by 'Street ' and includes the words ' of ', and also those whose address starts by 'Avenue '.

What to do: you can use operator LIKE (e.g. textAttribute LIKE 'Words%OtherWords?', where % means any number of characters of any type, and ? means any single character).

Answer 2.

Select firstName, lastName, address

From consultants

Where address like 'Street % of %' or address like 'Avenue %';

Exercise 3.

Show all attributes of tasks of projects 1 and 5.

Answer 3.
Select *
From task
Where projectID=1 or projectID=5;

Exercise 4.
Show all distinct jobs of consultants.

What to do: apply a keyword DISTINCT in the SELECT clause.

Answer 4.
Select distinct job
From consultant;

Exercise 5.
Show the projectID, title and description of all tasks whose planned budget is between 100,000 and 200,000, in descending order of planned budget.

Answer 5:
Select projectID, title, description
From task
Where budgetplanned between 100,000 and 200,000
Order by budgetplanned desc;

Or

Select projectID, title, description
From task
Where budgetplanned >= 100000 and budgetplanned <= 200000
Order by budgetplanned desc;

Exercise 6.
Show all tasks that are currently running (title, startDate, endDate).

Answer 6.

Select title, startDate, endDate

From task

Where now()>=startDate and now()<endDate;

Note: the function to get the current date depends on the R-DBMS. For instance, now() is valid in postgreSQL™, while it should be replaced by sysdate in Oracle.

Exercise 7.

Show all tasks (projectID, taskNum, title) that already ended whose budget (reported) was above 100,000 and was overrun by at least 10% (budget overrun is computed as (planned budget – reported budget) / planned budget).

Answer 7.

Select projectID, taskNum, title

From Task

Where budgetreported > 100,000 and endDate < now()

     and (budgetreported- budgetplanned)/budgetplanned >= 0.1

4.4. Join Operations

Exercise 1.

Show the title, start date and end date of each task, together with the task manager (first name and last name), ordering the result by task start date.

Answer 1.

Select tile, startDate, endDate, firstName, lastName

From task, consultant

Where task.taskManager = consultant.consultantID

Order by startDate;

Exercise 2.

Show a list of all participations of consultants in tasks of project 1. The list must include the task number, title of the task, its start date, its end date, the first name and last name of the consultant, the date the consultant started working on the task and the date when he ended work on the task.

Answer 2.

```
Select      taskNum, title, task.startDate, task.endDate,
            firstName, lastName,
            c.startDate, c.startDate + numberOfDays as endDate
From Consultants c, Task t, TaskConsultant tc
Where       c.consultantID=tc.consultantID
            and tc.taskNum=t.taskNum
            and tc.projectID=t.projectID
            and t.projectID=1;
```

Exercise 3.

Find all supervisors of consultants. Show the result organized as tuples with the values <FirstName, LastName, Supervisor FirstName, Supervisor LastName>.

What to do: you need to do a "self-join" of relation Consultant with itself. The second Consultant relation participating in the join is the Supervisor relation, but it happens that the supervisor is also a consultant, therefore the Supervisor relation is the Consultant relation.

Answer3.

```
Select c.firstName as FirstName, c.lastName as LastName,
            s.firstName as "Supervisor FirstName",
            s.lastName as "Supervisor LastName"
From Consultant c, Consultant s
Where c.supervisorID=s.consultantID;
```

Exercise 4.

Repeat the previous query, but this time make sure that senior consultants (those without a supervisor|) are also shown.

What to do: Consultants without supervisors have a null value in the "supervisorID" field. You need to use a FULL OUTER JOIN, or at least a LEFT OUTER JOIN, to make sure that tuples that do not match are represented in the result.

Answer 4.
Select c.firstName as FirstName, c.lastName as LastName,
       s.firstName as "Supervisor FirstName",
       s.lastName as "Supervisor LastName"
Consultant c FULL OUTER JOIN Consultant s
       ON (c.supervisorID=s.consultantID);

4.5. Cartesian Product, Union and Difference

Exercise 1.
Show all possible combinations of consultant names (firstName, lastName), using a Cartesian product.

Answer 1.
Select c.firstName, c.lastName, c2.firstName, c2.lastName
From Consultant c, Consultant c2;

Exercise 2.
Show, in the same output, consultants whose job is Manager and those whose job is Junior Consultant. The output should show the names and the job. Do this in two ways: the first is by using a disjunctive condition on the WHERE clause, the second is by using a UNION operator.

Answer 2.
Select firstName, lastName, job
From Consultant
Where job='Manager' or job='Junior Consultant';

Or

Select firstName, lastName, job
From Consultant
Where job='Manager'
UNION
Select firstName, lastName, job
From Consultant
Where job='Junior Consultant';

4.6. Aggregations

Aggregation functions compute useful aggregate quantities from the data, and those aggregates may be obtained per groups (GROUP BY). They are easy to use, and especially useful to obtain statistics about the distribution of the underlying data. The simplest example is to compute statistics (for instance, an average, a maximum and a minimum) of some variable. The following example computes the average, maximum and minimum hourly rate. The result is a single row with the three values.

SELECT avg(hourlyRate), max(hourlyRate), min(hourlyRate)
FROM Consultant;

This basic capability is further extended by the Group-By construct. The idea is that we may want to compute those statistics per group based on some property that groups individuals. For instance, if we want the same statistics per job, we need to submit the following query,

SELECT avg(hourlyRate), max(hourlyRate), min(hourlyRate), job
FROM Consultant
GROUP BY job;

Furthermore, if we want to restrict the results to some subset of the groups, all we need to do is to add a HAVING clause with a predicate restricting which groups will be included in the result, such as in,

SELECT avg(hourlyRate), max(hourlyRate), min(hourlyRate), job
FROM Consultant
GROUP BY job

HAVING job='Manager'

We can also use expressions, such as,

SELECT sum(hourlyRate + commission) / count(*)
FROM Consultant;

4.6.1. Examples of Aggregation Functions

AVG(attribute | expression) – compute the average;

COUNT(attribute | *) – computes the number of tuples. If * is used, all tuples are considered, if attribute is used, tuples with null value for the attribute are not considered;

MAX(attribute | expression), MIN(attribute | expression) – computes the maximum or the minimum value of an attribute or of some expression;

SUM(attribute | expression) – computes the sum of values;

STDDEV(attribute | expression), VARIANCE(attribute | expression) – computes the standard deviation or the variance;

PERCENTILE(attribute | expression, p) – computes the pth percentile of the distribution given by the values taken by an attribute or expression;

4.6.2.Exercises

Exercise 1.
Show the number of consultants for each job (Job, How Many).

Answer 1.
Select job, count(*) as "How Many"
From Consultant
Group by job;

Exercise 2.
Show how many consultants have no supervisor.

Answer 2.

Select count(*)

From Consultant

Where supervisorID is NULL;

Exercise 3.

Determine how much task 1 of project 1 had to pay to each consultant. Show the result as (consultantID, lastName, firstName, owed).

Answer 3.

Select   c.consultantID, c.lastName, c.firstName,
                sum(numberOfDays * hourlyRate) as owed

From TaskConsultant tc, Consultant c

Where tc.consultantID=c.consultantID

And taskNum=1 and projectID=1

Group by c.consultantID, c.lastName, c.firstName;

Exercise 4.

Determine how much each project had to pay to each consultant. Show the result as (consultantID, lastName, firstName, project, payed).

Answer 4.

Select   c.consultantID, c.lastName, c.firstName, projectName,
                sum(numberOfDays * hourlyRate) as payed

From TaskConsultant tc, Consultant c, Project p

Where tc.consultantID=c.consultantID

And tc.projectID=p.projectID

Group by c.consultantID, c.lastName, c.firstName, projectName;

Exercise 5.

Determine the total amount owed to consultant with last name 'Clark' and first name 'John' between the beginning of 2010 and today. Show the result as (total).

Answer 5.

Select sum(numberOfDays * hourlyRate) as total

From TaskConsultant tc, Consultant c
Where tc.consultantID=c.consultantID
And lastName='Clark'
And startDate >=to_date('2010-01-01','yyyy-mm-dd');

Exercise 6.
Find the most expensive planned budget, the average planned budget, the standard deviation of planned budget and the least costly planned budget from all tasks.

Answer 6.
Select   max(budgetPlanned), average(budgetPlanned),
            stdev(budgetPlanned), min(budgetPlanned)
from task;

Exercise 7.
Repeat the previous query, but this time compute the same statistics but per project. Show the project Name and ID in the result.

Answer 7.
Select   max(budgetPlanned), average(budgetPlanned),
            stdev(budgetPlanned), min(budgetPlanned),
            projectName, projectID
from task
Where task.projectID=project.projectID
Group by projectName, projectID;

Challenge Exercise 8.
Find the maximum, minimum and average income per job in task 1 of project 1. Show only those jobs with income above 5,000, and order the result by average income in decreasing order.

4.7. Subqueries

Assume that we want to list information about the tasks of a project with project name 'Information System of Airport XY'. The following query is submitted:

```
SELECT taskNum, title
FROM task
WHERE projectID =
            Select projectID
            From project
            Where projectName='Information System of Airport XY';
```

This query has a subquery in it. The subquery gets the projectID, which is used in the outer query.

It is frequently possible to write different SQL queries that obtain the same result. In this case, we can use a join instead of a sub-query. The query would be written as,

```
SELECT taskNum, title
FROM task, project
WHERE task.projectID = project.projectID
AND projectName='Information System of Airport XY';
```

Another formulation would use a subquery in the FROM clause. Remember that the FROM clause specifies relations, which are sets of tuples. Since queries return relations themselves, we can replace the name of a relation by any query in the FROM clause. Then we need to take adequate care of joins in the query. The previous query could be written as,

```
SELECT taskNum, title
FROM task, ( Select projectID From project
      Where projectName='Information System of Airport XY' ) as p
WHERE projectID = p.projectID;
```

In this case we created a temporary relation named p with the result of the inner query, then we did the join between relations task and p based on the attribute projectID of both.

4.7.1.Exercises

The following are a few additional exercises with subqueries and aggregations as well. You should specify the query in a single text.

Exercise 1.
Use a single query to show the number of consultants of each job with hourly rates above the average (Job, How Many).

Answer 1.
Select job, count(*) "How Many"
From consultant
Where   hourlyRate >
          Select avg(hourlyRate) from consultant;

Exercise 2.
Show all tasks whose planned budget is above the average planned budget.

Answer 2.
Select projectID, taskNum, title, budgetplanned
From task
Where budgetplanned >
          Select avg(budgetplanned) from task;

Exercise 3.
Find the consultant who earned more money in project 1.
Show the result as (FirstName, LastName).

Answer 3.
Select firstName, lastName
From Consultant c,
          (Select sum(numberOfDays) * hourlyRate * 8 as earned,
              c.consultantID as consultantID
          From Consultant c, TaskConsultant tc
              Where c.consultantID=tc.consultantID
              and projectID=1
) as income

Where c.consultantID= income.consultantID
and earned =

> Select max(earned)
> From
> (Select sum(numberOfDays) * hourlyRate * 8 as earned,
> > c.consultantID as consultant
> > From Consultant c, TaskConsultant tc
> > Where c.consultantID=tc.consultantID
> > And projectID=1
>) ;

Exercise 4.
Find all tasks where Consultant 'John Clark' participated. Do this using the three alternatives (a single-level query, using a sub-query of the WHERE clause and using a sub-query of the FROM clause).

Answer 4.
Select t.projectID, t.taskNum, t.title
From task t, taskConsultant tc, Consultant c
Where t.taskNum=tc.taskNum and t.projectID=tc.projectID
And tc.consultantID=c.consultantID
And firstName='John' and lastName='Clark';

Or

Select t.projectID, t.taskNum, t.title
From task t, taskConsultant tc
Where t.taskNum=tc.taskNum and t.projectID=tc.projectID
and tc.consultantID=

> (Select consultantID
>   From Consultant
>   Where firstName='John' and lastName='Clark');

Or

Select t.projectID, t.taskNum, t.title
From task t, taskConsultant tc,
> (Select consultantID

From Consultant
Where firstName='John'
And lastName='Clark') as JohnClark
Where t.taskNum=tc.taskNum and t.projectID=tc.projectID
and tc.consultantID=JohnClark.consultantID;

Exercise 5.

Find how much each consultant earned in each project. Report the results as (Project, LastName, Amount Earned).

Answer 5.

Select tc.projectID, c.lastName, c.hourlyRate * 8 * numberOfdays
From taskConsultant tc, Consultant c,
(select projectID, consultantID, sum(numberOfDays) as numberOfdays
  from taskConsultant
  group by projectID, consultantID
) as projectParticipation
where tc. consultantID= c.consultantID
and tc. projectID = projectParticipation.projectID
and tc.consultantID = projectParticipation.consultantID;

Challenge Exercise 6.

Find the consultants who earned more money in each project. Report the results as (Project, LastName, Amount Earned).

Pedro Furtado

5. Entity-Relationship Model

Database projects start by considering the real-world problem for which an information system is needed, and by describing the needs of that information system. In this context, the database is the computerized entity that will store and manage data, and the information system is the pair made of the database and the applications that handle the data and interface with users and other systems. Typical data applications include user interfaces, for user interaction, and application logic, for data manipulation.

The relational and entity-relationship models are related to the database part of the project, in the sense that they are used to determine the exact structure of the data that will be stored persistently in the database engine. But they are also related to the applications that handles the data, since the structure of the data is designed to be manipulated by applications with specific objectives.

The entity–relationship (ER) model was proposed by Peter Chen in [4]. It is expected to capture important semantics about some real world problem. Chen also proposed a diagrammatic technique for database design using the model and an example of database design and description. Since then, the ER model and modeling techniques have evolved substantially.

We start by summarizing the strength of Entity-Relationship (ER) models, and then its limitations when compared to object-oriented models. Then we describe in great detail how to design an ER model, and how to transform it into a relational model after the ER has been designed. Designers may use variations and slightly different ways to think about the design, we concentrated on providing a fairly detailed tutorial about how to reason in order to arrive at a good representation.

5.1. Strength of Entity-Relationship Model

The Entity-Relationship or ER model was proposed in [4]. The objective of the ER model is to reason about the database schema (a set of entities and relationships) at a conceptual (logical) level, without having to deal with the lower-level details of relations and references (sometimes called the physical model). Designers resort to the conceptual model to help thinking about the problem at the level of concepts (abstractions).

As the name itself implies, the Entity-Relationship model defines two main concepts, the Entity and the Relationship. It requires information systems designers to express the real-world problem as a set of entities and relationships between those entities. This is a convenient representation for real-world things, such as cars and houses, or students and teachers. Students and Teachers are entities, and they share the relationship that the teacher teaches the students.

Besides providing an intuitive way to design a database schema, one major strength of the ER model is that there are systematic rules to transform it into a relational model (R) automatically, or at least semi-automatically. There are computerized database design tools that allow you to design the ER model for the particular problem you are dealing with, and then use automated ER-R conversion to derive a relational (R) diagram. These tools most frequently also do Relational to SQL (R-SQL/DDL) conversion, producing the SQL statements that create the schema in a target database engine. This way, you can design the ER and generate the SQL commands to create the database just be clicking the right buttons.

5.1. Entity-Relationship and Relational versus Object Orientation

ER models are perfect for designing database schemas that will be represented as relations. However, both ER and R models are poorer than object-oriented models in how they represent many real-world objects. For instance, consider one person with a set of children. This can easily be represented in object-oriented models exactly as stated, as an object (Person) that has an attribute named children, which is a set of Person objects, as represented in Figure 16 (the set is represented as [objects] in the figure),

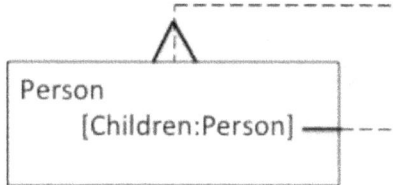

Person(name:String, children[child:Person],...)

Figure 16 – A Person with Children in an OO Model

In an Entity-Relationship model, the same object must be represented as an entity and a relationship, which translates into two relations in the relational model, as shown in Figure 17.

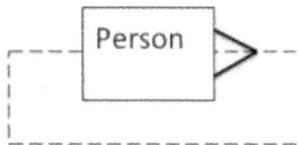

Person(name:String,...)
Children(parent:Person, child:Person)

Figure 17 – A Person with Children in ER model and as Relations

"Children" represents a relationship between two persons in the entity-relationship model, and is represented in the relational model as a relation.

The previous discussion has shown that object-orientation allow programmers to represent everything as objects, while relational databases (and the entity-relationship model) require some transformations to represent some of the concepts. This limitation has attracted a lot of attention from researchers, who investigated the use of object orientation for modeling and representing database schemas. They have created database object-oriented models, object-oriented database engines, object-relational mappings and approaches to translate automatically between objects and relations, such as by using Hybernate [12][13]. Hybernate™ is an object-relational mapping framework for Java™, mapping objects in object-oriented applications to relational database relations. Hibernate replaces direct database accesses with high-level object handling methods.

There was some hype around those concepts during the 90's of the previous century, including many commercial ventures, but contrary to the most successful relational database companies, they did not find a significant market for their products. Even object-relational extensions that exist in some main commercial database engines are seldom used in information systems of organizations.

These hard facts seem to indicate that relational databases, relational models and the ER model are well-suited for everyday information systems. We can list some of the possible reasons for that:

1. The schema is usually simple to understand when expressed as ER models, since there are only entities and relationships between entities, entities and attributes are not nested;

2. ER and R models are sufficiently powerful to represent the data that needs to be stored for those applications;

3. It is very easy to write queries that the application needs declaratively using SQL, there is no nesting or other complex navigation between entities;

4. Relational technology provides an adequate separation between the data schema and the application logic (the data schema "lives" independently of applications using it);

5. When application-developers want to use objects instead of relations and references, programming frameworks that include object-relational mapping functionality translate automatically between relations and objects;

There are, however, specialized applications where object-oriented databases can be advantageous, for instance in Geographical Information Systems (GIS), and the future may bring new advances in the relationship between object-orientation, databases and database modeling.

5.2. Defining the Entity-Relationship Model

Given a real-world problem for which we want to develop an information system, the database should be designed starting from an ER diagram. There exist multiple design choices when creating an ER diagram, but it should be possible to state whether one design is good or not. A good design is one that represents the real-world entities and relationships well, and that is well-structured for representing the data that needs to be represented, and also for data manipulation in a database.

The first step in defining the ER model is to describe the information system that needs to be built by writing. The description should be an informal text. However, it should be made of well-separated paragraphs, try to be as complete and systematic as possible in what concerns the main requirements, and it should specify all important facts that need to be taken into account. Some details may be missing, and the designers may have to make choices along the design process concerning those missing details. That in turn will help further define the requirements. The real-world problem is described from the point of view of the information system. This can be seen as a "Requirements Elicitation" phase.

We will use three examples of "real-world" problems next to show how the various steps of the design process should work. The first step is to contextualize the problem, which we do next with a short description of the problem to be solved.

5.2.1.Example 1. A Database of Projects

An engineering company develops projects for customers. The company has a set of consultants. Senior consultants search for business opportunities and setup projects with customers. The project is defined as a set of tasks, and other consultants participate in the project as human resources. The company wants to have a database to track the projects and participation of consultants in projects.

Example 1 – Description of Intended Information System: A Database of Projects

The database must store information about projects.

For each project, the database must represent the customer and tasks of the project.

For each task, there must be information about consultants that participate in the task.

One (senior) Consultant is the Project Manager. This is most frequently the person who sets up the project with a customer.

Projects have a numerical ID, an acronym, a description, and indication of the location where it will take place, start and end dates, customer and budgetary information.

The budgetary information that needs to be recorded for a project is the planned budget (the amount negotiated with the customer) and the actual budget (actual money spent until the current day).

Both in what concerns dates and budget, we want to keep track of planned and actual values, so that we will be able to detect problems with plans or with the project itself.

When a project is planned, its tasks must be entered into the system. A task is identified by an ordinal number (starting by 1), and a title. For instance, task 1 of the project might be to setup some infrastructure for the rest of the project, and it might be called "Infrastructure Setup".

Customers can be individuals or companies. Customers have an identification (name or company name), an address, a primary and secondary contact person and also a primary and secondary phone number. It is necessary to record the fiscal number of the customer. Other information about the customer includes its size, in number of employees (for companies). There should be a field for observations about the customer.

Besides the identifier and the title, tasks include a description text, and a text describing needs of the task.

Tasks must record planned and actual start and end dates, as well as planned and actual budget. The planned budget is defined upfront, when the project is being planned, and the actual budget is updated along the project. Besides a total budget, the per-task budget is also cut down into the following budget parcels – Human Resources (HR), Equipment, Consumables, Travel and Overheads.

Tasks also record human resource requirements in terms of man-month units (MM). There should be two MM fields: planned and current. When the task is being planned, the planned MM field is filled, and the planned HR budget is deduced from the planning.

It is very important to keep both panned and actual budgetary, dates and human resources data for tasks, so that we can detect any potential problems, dates and cost overruns in tasks.

The database must hold information about consultants. It is necessary to record the first name, last name and middle name of the consultant, together with his address, contact phone number and his job. The database must also record the start and end date for his collaboration with the company, and Bio information in textual format. The Bio includes Expertise and Curriculum. Finally, there should also be a field with his hourly rate (how much the consultant should earn per hour worked in a project) and another one holding his commission (a percentage of the negotiated budget that he earns for projects that he was able to setup with a customer, upon successful completion of the project).

For each task and each consultant that worked in that task, we would also like to know when he started and ended his work in the task, and the effort he put in it (measured as Man-Months), which will define his pay concerning that task.

First Draft and Arity

For the first sketch of an ER diagram, you do not need a computer. A very good way to design an initial Entity-Relationship (ER) diagram is by drawing a draft on a sheet of paper, indicating the major entities and relationships. In this initial draft, entities are rectangles with the name of the entity as label, relationships are connectors linking two entities. For each relationship, you should indicate its name and arity. As with entities, the name of the relationship should elucidate about what it represents. It is sometimes advocated that the name should be a verb. We prefer not to be so restrictive, since verbs will be repetitive. If the semantics of the relationship is obvious, a concatenation of the labels of entities, or prefixes of those labels, with or without a verb connector, is a good option. For instance, a Project has Tasks, therefore the relationship of Project and Task is projTasks, or it can be projHasTasks. In general, it is a good idea to name each relationship, since that name can be associated later with constraints or relations that represent the relationship in the physical diagram.

The arity is a very important and simultaneously intuitive concept in ER diagrams. A Project has multiple tasks, and a task is of a single project. This means that Project to Task is a 1:n relationship, where one Project can be associated with many tasks. The arity of the relationship is 1:n. Figure 18 shows alternative representations for this relationship arity. Notice where the (n) or trident symbol is placed: if a project is associated with multiple tasks, then the (n) or the trident is represented in the side of the task (one project to many tasks). We will use (a) most of the times.

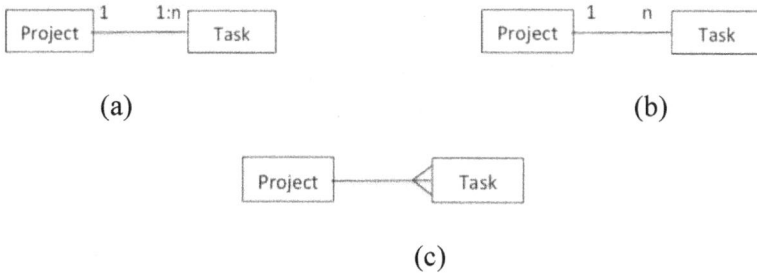

Figure 18. Project-Task Relationship arity: Alternatives

The relationship between Task and Consultant is an example of an n:n arity. One consultant may participate in multiple tasks (he can participate in multiple tasks in some project, and he can also participate in multiple tasks of different projects). Figure 19 represents that n:n relationship.

Figure 19. Task-Consultant Relationship

Example 1 – Design of the First Entity-Relationship Diagram: A Database of Projects

For this example, after reading the description of the intended information system, we define the entities and relationships as follows:

The entity Project has a Customer (Customer 1:n Project, since we consider that a Project has a single Customer). Notice that, in some real world case, it would be possible that a project be adjudicated to multiple customers, therefore it is useful to ask questions. When nothing is said, we should assume the most common semantics, and then check with the clients of the information system;

The entity Project has many tasks (Project 1:n Task, since we consider that a Task belongs to a single Project). Notice that, in some real world case, it would be possible for a task to be associated with more than one project. Nothing is said about that, we should assume the most common semantics;

The entity Task can have the participation of many Consultants, and a Consultant can participate in many tasks of the same or different projects (Task n:n Consultant);

One specific Consultant is the Project Manager (Consultant 1:n Project, since we consider that a Project has a single Project Manager).

This analysis results in the diagram of Figure 20.

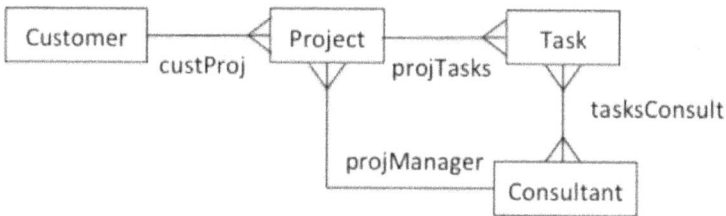

Figure 20. Draft Entity-Relationship Diagram for Projects Database

Optionality of Relationships

Another detail that is usually included in the analysis of the ER diagram is the optionality of relationships on each side. We investigate whether each entity is obliged to participate in the relationship or not. Consider an entity as a relation in the relational model, or equivalently, as a table in a database. We will denote each tuple of the relation or row of the table as an instance of the entity. For instance, if the entity is Person, the tuple containing data about you will be an instance of the relation. When analyzing optionality, the question that should be answered is: given a relationship AB between entities A and B, and given that an instance of entity A is inserted in the database, does it need to be associated with an inserted instance of entity B? If so, A has mandatory participation in relationship AB, otherwise it has optional participation.

Figure 21 illustrates the specification of mandatory and optional participation, using two different notations. Consider that a Project can have no tasks associated with it. In (a) the optional participation of Project is specified by indicating the 0 in the 0:n, as the degree of participation. If the participation was mandatory, 0:n should be replaced by 1:n. The same n-arity optional participation is indicated using a circle in the notation of (b), where the circle indicates optional (0:) and the trident indicates multiple (:n). On the other side of the same relationship in Figure 21, either a 1 or the vertical bar indicates mandatory participation (1 means there must be exactly one project associated with a task).

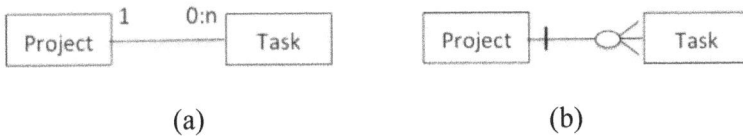

(a)   (b)

Figure 21. Examples of Mandatory and Optional Participation in Relationships

How do we decide whether a participation should be mandatory or optional in this case? We can ask the question of whether we can insert a new Project without having to insert the tasks of the project simultaneously. If we should be able to add a new project to the database without having to add its tasks, then the participation of entity Project in relationship projTask is optional, otherwise it is mandatory. From the perspective of tasks, we can ask the question of whether it would make sense to be able to add a task without associating it with a project. If we always have to associate a task with a project when we insert the task, Task has mandatory participation in the relationship, otherwise it has optional participation.

In our example we should be able to add general information of a project (the Project entity) without having to specify the details of tasks of the project (Task entity). Therefore, Project has optional participation in the relationship. On the other hand, when we are inserting a new task, since it belongs to a specific project that we should already have defined, it should be mandatory to relate that task with a project. This rationale results in the arity and optionality of Figure 21.

Not all optionality choices have a single correct answer. It is natural for some participations to be either optional or mandatory depending on choices of the designer. It should however be clear to the designer how those choices will affect user interactions and user interfaces of applications using the database. For instance, if we specify that a project has mandatory participation in the relationship with tasks, then the user interface must oblige the user to create/associate at least one task with the project when he creates a new project, or more precisely when he hits the button that triggers insertion of the new project into the database. Likewise, if participation of tasks in projects is mandatory, when the user specifies a task, the user interface must allow the user to associate that task with a project, and he is obliged to do so.

Example 1 – Refinement of the Entity-Relationship Diagram: A Database of Projects

Customers may be added to the information system without being associated with any project, although they should later be associated with some project(s). This accounts for the optional participation of entity Customer in relationship *custProj* of Figure 22.

Projects must always be associated with some customer, who is also responsible for paying the project. This accounts for the mandatory participation of Project in custProj relationship of Figure 22.

A Project may or may not have tasks associated with it. When a project is registered initially, we can insert its title, description, customer and many other information, without immediately describing its tasks. Later on we will insert its tasks, as we plan the project and its budget. This accounts for the optional participation of entity Project in relationship projTasks.

A task registered in the database must be associated with a specific project. This accounts for the mandatory participation of Task in projTasks relationship.

A task may have no consultant, and a consultant can be registered without the need to associate him/her to any task. This accounts for the optionality on both sides of the taskConsult relationship.

A consultant may also not be associated with any project when it is first inserted into the database, but a project always has a project manager, since it is the project manager that is responsible also for setting up the project. This accounts for the optional and mandatory characteristics of the sides of relationship projManager.

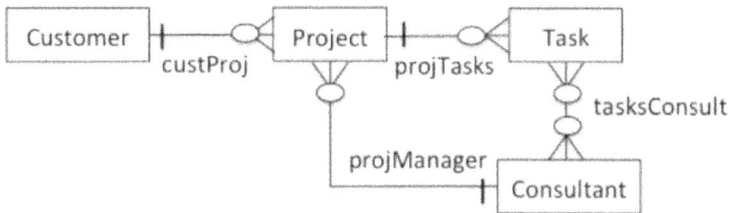

Figure 22. ER Diagram for Projects, with Arity and Optionality

5.2.2.Example 2 - Food Factory Quality Control Database

The problem (short initial description): A food company manufactures baby food products, which are then packaged and sold all over the world. The company wants to develop a quality control database for its factories. Each factory buys raw ingredients from suppliers, such as flour, milk, eggs and many others. The database is meant to detect when a product or batch of products produced does not meet quality standards, locate the origin of the problem, withdraw the products likely to be affected, eliminate raw ingredients that might have caused the problem and pinpoint faulty suppliers.

Example 2 – Description of Intended Information System: Food Factory Quality Control Database

The information system records production information.

Raw ingredients are supplied to the factory in individual packages with an identification code, or in large containers with many packages and also a container identification code.

Batches of raw material are made of raw ingredients dumped from supplied packages or containers. Information about the packages or containers that make up a raw material batch is recorded in the information system when they enter production.

Products are produced in production batches, and packaged into individual packages or containers. Containers have multiple packages. The information system should keep record of every such container and package.

Quality control is based on analyzing and tasting samples of end products and raw ingredients. When a problem is detected, all ingredients and products that may be related to the problem are removed, or at least analyzed carefully.

In order to enforce this quality control, the database must record which raw material batches were used in the production of which product batches. Production information keeps track of the product batches. For a production batch we identify the raw materials batches used in its production (multiple raw materials – ingredients - are used). This information allows quality control operators to find containers, packages or batches of products and of raw materials that should be removed when a quality problem is detected with a package of a final product.

There will be many suppliers registered in the database, and the raw materials are associated with respective suppliers, to be able to identify who supplied a certain container or package. Supplier records have identification (company name), fiscal number, address, a primary and secondary contact person and also primary and secondary phone contact numbers. Other information about suppliers includes the size, measured in number of employees, and textual fields to record observations.

In the production line, the system automatically records the batch number, containers and packages of raw materials as soon as those materials enter production, along with a timestamp of entry. It also registers each output product batch, container and package, along with the timestamp, and associates raw material batches with product batches, allowing a trace-back from output product to the batches, containers and packages of corresponding raw materials.

When it is necessary to eliminate problematic products and raw materials, the information system must allow the quality control employees to trace back which batches, containers and packages of raw materials were associated with the defective end product. All the information regarding defective products and corresponding raw materials is recorded and kept in the information system. Quality control employees will be able to know exactly which product packages, containers and batches were problematic, which were removed from commercialization, which raw materials (packages, containers, batches) were used in the production of those products, and who were the suppliers of those raw materials. Conversely, when analysis of a raw ingredient detects problems, it should be possible to trace which products used those raw materials.

Example 2 – Entity-Relationship Diagram: Food Factory Quality Control Database

Based on the previous description, Figure 23 shows a possible ER diagram for the problem. In the figure, entities 'Raw Material Unit' and 'Product Unit' represent individual parts that are inputs and outputs of the production respectively. They have a 'Product Type' associated with each, and they can be either containers or packages. Moreover, containers are made of many packages, which is also represented in the figure by the relationship between containers and packages.

In Figure 23, batches of raw materials and batches of products are each made of a set of raw material units and product units respectively. The relationship ProdRawBatch associates batches of raw materials with batches of products. It indicates which product batches were made with which raw material batches.

The ER (conceptual diagram) will be transformed into a relational (physical) diagram. However, at this point, we should not be worried about which relations will result from the entities and relationships, and there is not a one-one relationship between entities and relations when transforming from ER to relational. For instance, although we define entities for containers and packages, it does not mean that we will have relations for representing each, perhaps we can decide to have only the "Unit" relations, with an attribute that identifies whether it is a container or a package. Those decisions are taken later on, based on a more detailed analysis of attributes and relationships.

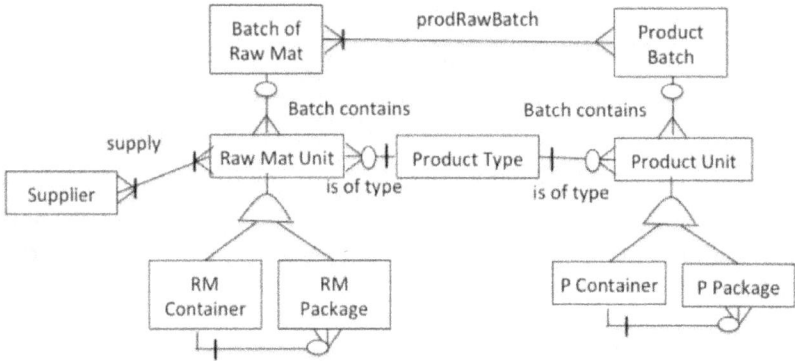

Figure 23. ER Model of Food Factory Quality Control Database - I

The two sides of the diagram of Figure 23 are similar, because a raw material can also be considered a (raw) product. An alternative diagram shown in Figure 24 represents production as a transformation of products into other products, where raw materials are also products. We can include an attribute indicating if the product is a raw material or a finished product. Both diagrams are valid.

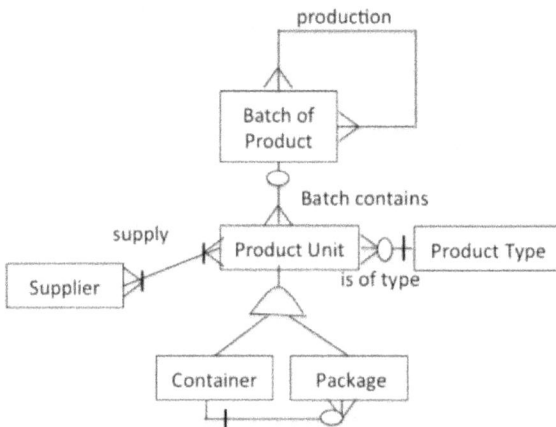

Figure 24. ER Model of Food Factory Quality Control Database - II

5.2.3.Example 3. Clinical Information Database

Example 3 – Entity-Relationship Diagram: Clinical Information Database for an Hospital

The problem: A Clinical Information System is needed which must track patient visits to the hospital. Those are either emergency visits, previously-booked appointments or overnight stays. An emergency visit can lead to extended overnight stays. Patient, date, time and other details should be filled regarding the hospital visit event.

The tracking of patient clinical information is done by means of recording "clinical episodes", which should be linked to the relevant hospital visit event (one hospital visit event can be related to multiple clinical episodes), and to the medical doctor who observed the patient in that clinical episode. The medical doctor records symptoms and diagnosis hypothesis, as well as any diagnostic exams that may take place.

Clinical observation exams are just descriptions of what the medical doctor observed, while blood chemical analysis and imaging exams are complementary exams that may be requested as well. A "Bio Indicators" table identifies different bio parameters (e.g. cholesterol) and the interval of values considered normal for that bio parameter. Actual measurements are recorded as Bio Measurements of a specific exam, related to the corresponding bio indicators. The imaging exam is any exam that is based on imaging procedures. In that case, the raw image and any observations about the image are recorded.

Given this description, Figure 25 shows the corresponding ER diagram.

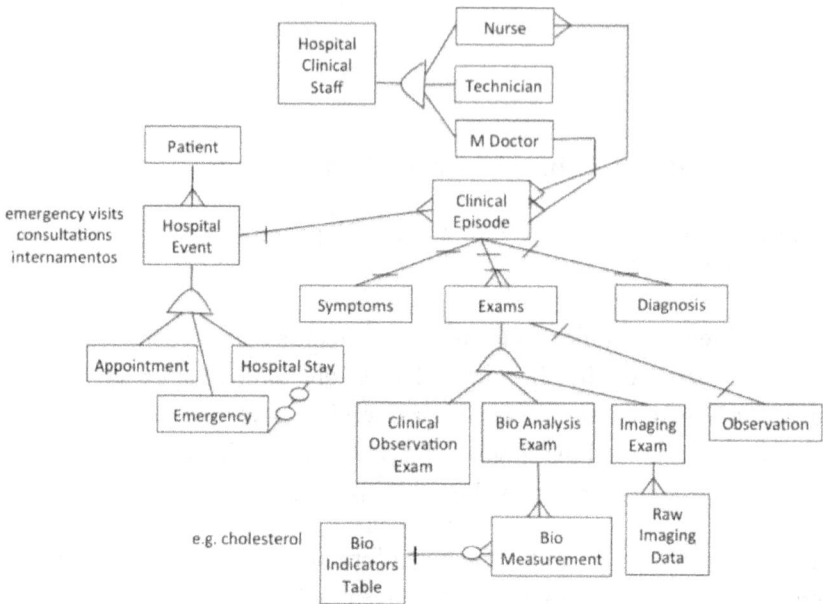

Figure 25. ER Model for the Hospital Clinical Information Database

5.3. Identifiers

When a stable version of the initial ER diagram is obtained, the next step is to think about the attributes of entities and relationships, and also of unique identifiers of entities.

When we studied the relational model in previous chapters, we discussed primary keys and foreign keys. Foreign keys are references to other relations. In an ER diagram there should be no foreign keys in an entity, or any kind of reference to other entities inside an entity. It is a common mistake to add such references. An entity can only describe itself, and it cannot include any type of information about a related entity or any kind of reference to another entity. The only way to relate two entities is using relationships. Foreign keys are derived from relationships when the relational diagram is generated from the ER diagram.

It is therefore a necessary condition for an ER diagram to be consistent that any entity does not contain any information concerning other entities of the same ER. Very often the mistake is committed of adding attributes to an entity in the ER that are actually "fake" references to other entities. For instance, a "Project" is related to a "Customer" in the Projects database of Figure 20, and a "Clinical Episode" is related to an "Hospital Visit Event" in Figure 25. The Project entity cannot have a customerID attribute or the name of the customer of the project. The first case (customerID) is a "fake" foreign key. It is called "fake" because the designer did not understand that he is in fact wrongly indicating a foreign key, which is redundant with the relationship between Project and Customer. The second case – including the name of the customer as an attribute of Project – is also inconsistent with the diagram of Figure 20, since there is a Customer entity and a relationship with it, therefore the name of the customer should not be placed in the Project entity.

The only way the name of the customer could make sense in the Project entity would be if there was no Customer entity at all. The Customer entity is needed if we have multiple attributes in Customer (e.g. address, contacts, size), to better organize the data and to avoid anomalies that result from repeating the same data (e.g. the address and contacts of the customer when more than one project is done for the same customer).

While entities cannot have (fake) references to other entities, they need identifiers. Therefore, the next important step is to define the identifiers of each entity.

Figure 26 shows the same entity-relationship diagram of Figure 20 but now we added identifiers to each entity. The identifier (primary key) must distinguish instances of the entity uniquely. We have the choice to either create an artificial identifier, or to use some attribute that already identifies the instances uniquely. In this case we have chosen: customer social security number (custSSN), to identify customers uniquely; the social security number was also chosen for consultants (consSSN); a project number (projN) for projects; and a task number (taskN) for tasks. The attribute projN is an artificial identifier, since we will assign incrementing integers to that identifier, starting by the value 1. The attribute taskN is also artificial and ordinal, in the sense that it orders project tasks incrementally.

There is also a new symbol in the diagram, the dependency relationship symbol, illustrated in Figure 27. The task number (taskN) is not enough to identify a task uniquely, since different projects will have the same task number taskN. For instance, task number 1 exists in both project P1 and project P2. For that reason, TaskN alone would not be suitable as a primary key.

The dependency relationship exists to represent an identification dependency, in this case between Task and Project. What this means is that the dependent entity (Task in this case) is partly identified by the entity it depends on or, equivalently, that the identifier of the dependent entity (Task in the example) includes the identifier of the entity it depends from. The dependent entity (Task in the example) is also sometimes called "weak entity".

Given this definition, the identifier of Task will be (taskN, projN), but we do not indicate projN explicitly as an identifier of Task in the ER diagram of Figure 26, since that is implicit from the dependency relationship.

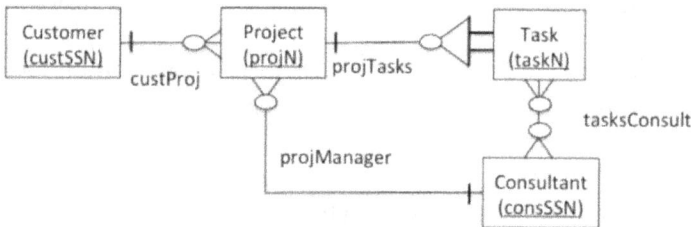

Figure 26. Entity-Relationship with Identifiers

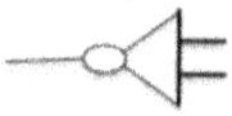

Figure 27. Dependency Relationship

Relationships may also have attributes associated with them. One example for Figure 26 is the indication of starting and ending dates for the participation of a consultant in a task, as shown in Figure 28. While the start and end dates of a task are properties of tasks, and the start and end dates of the collaboration of a consultant with the company can be added to entity Consultant, the start and end dates of the participation of a consultant in a specific task can only be placed as an attribute of the relationship between tasks and consultants.

To further clarify: the start and end dates of participation of consultants in tasks could not be part of entity Task, since there is one such pair of dates for each consultant that participates in each task. It could also not be part of consultant, because there is one such pair of dates for each task the consultant participates in. Consequently, it has to be a pair of attributes of the relationship.

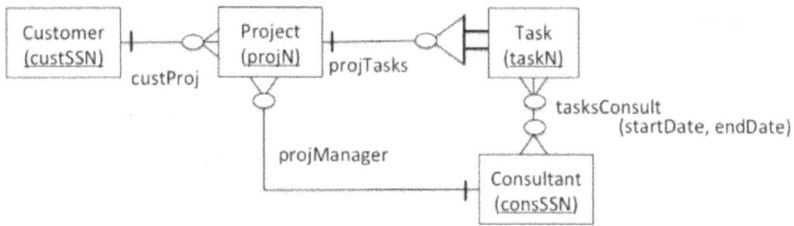

Figure 28. Projects Database – Relationship Attributes

Many-to-many (a.k.a. N:M) relationships can be transformed into an equivalent representation as weak entity with dependent relationships, as shown in Figure 29. While the M:N relationship of Figure 28 could be read as "a consultant can participate in multiple tasks, and a task can have multiple consultants working on it", the same relationship can be read in Figure 29 as "a taskConsult instance represents a participation of a consultant in a task. Both consultants and tasks can participate in multiple taskConsult instances". The identifier of the new taskConsult entity can be void, because this entity is dependent on both Task and Consultant (dependency relationship), which means that it "inherits" as identifier the identifiers of both entities of which it depends. Given that the identifier of Task is (projN, taskN), and the identifier of Consultant is (consSSN), the identifier of taskConsult will be (projN, taskN, consSSN). It means that a taskConsult instance relates a specific consultant (consSSN) to a specific task of a specific project (projN, taskN). As we already indicated before, we do not show inherited identifiers explicitly, therefore we do not show them in the taskConsult entity of Figure 29.

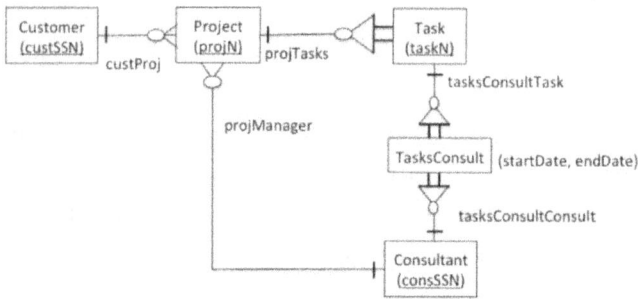

Figure 29. Projects Database – M:N Relationship as weak Entity

We may need to add attributes to the TasksConsult entity, and we may also have to add another identifier to the entity if a consultant can participate more than once in the same task in different date intervals. Assuming that we want to record multiple participations of the same consultant in a task as two separate instances, the triple (projN, taskN, consSSN) will not be enough to represent each individual participation independently, since the same consultant (consSSN) participates multiple times in the same task (projN, taskN).

Since we must guarantee uniqueness of instances, the solution is to add startDate to the identifier, resulting in the diagram of Figure 30.

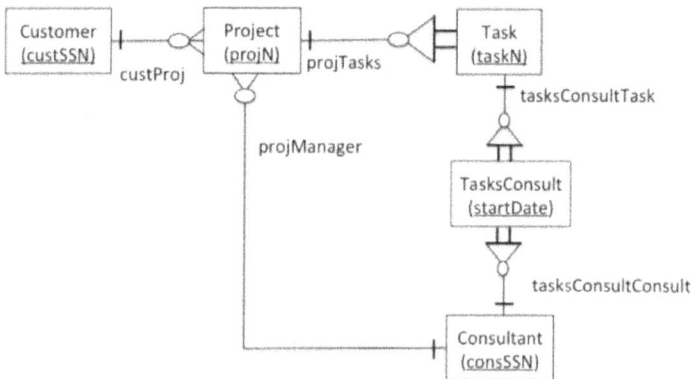

Figure 30. Projects Database – completing an identifier to M:N Relationship

Customers may be either individuals or companies. We have not represented the two alternatives before, so we change the ER diagram. Figure 31 shows the new version of the ER, with the two alternative customer types as children of the inheritance relationship with Customer. Notice that we do not add identifiers to the children in an inheritance. Since the children have the same type of the parent, they use the same identifier as the parent itself.

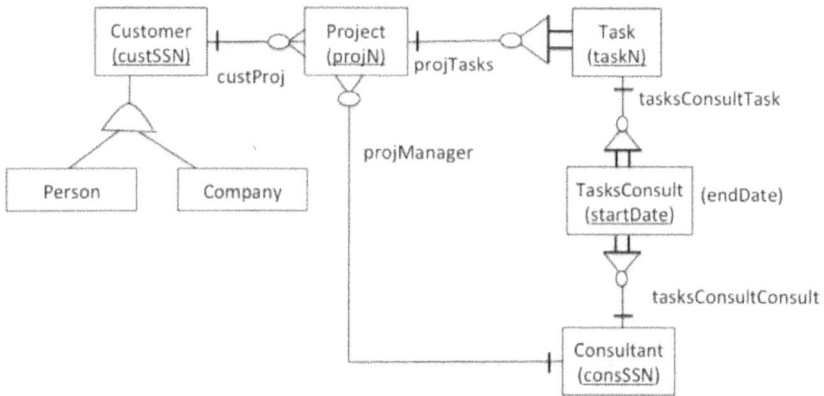

Figure 31. Projects Database - Customer Inheritance

5.4. Attributes

We also need to define all the attributes of entities. Attributes are the holders of all data that needs to be recorded about the entity. This is related to the requirements that are listed in the detailed description of the problem. We need to read the detailed description and check that every detail that needs to be recorded is represented as an attribute of some entity.

As we have seen in a previous chapter, attributes have domains, data types and constraints associated with them, which we should also add to the design.

Figure 32 shows entities Customer and Project, as well as the custProj relationship, with corresponding attributes and domains. You can see that entity Project has dates and budgetary information, and for each one, it keeps planned and actual values. This allows us to track whether the plan was accurate and whether there were problems with the project.

In the customer inheritance there are attributes common to both children entities. We should be able to identify attributes that both children share in common and represent them in the parent of the inheritance relationship. Figure 33 shows a refined version of part of the ER with that modification.

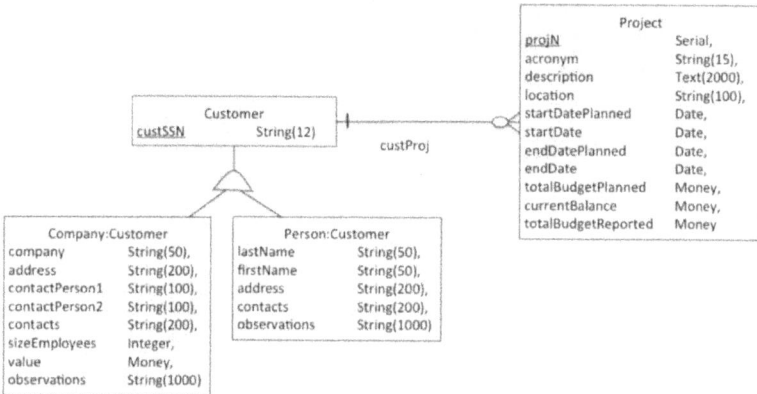

Figure 32. Project-Customer part of the Projects Database ER

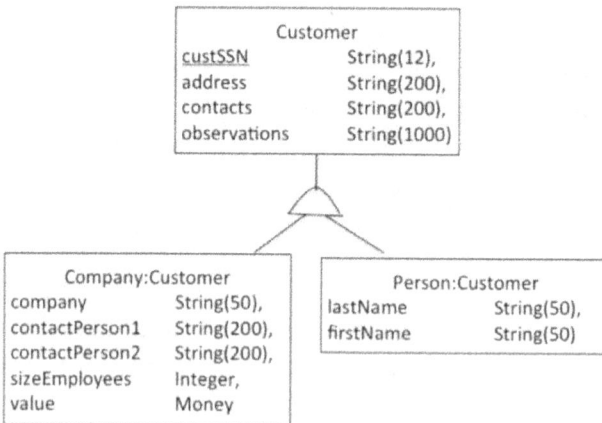

Figure 33. Refined Project-Customer part of the Projects Database ER

Figure 34 shows the attributes of the remaining entities of the Projects Database ER. Notice that attributes were included in tasks to record dates (planned and actual), budget (including total, human resources, equipment and consumables), total planned and actual effort in Man-Month (MM). This answers the requests stated in the requirements that the project tasks should include dates, budgetary and human resource needs.

In what concerns Consultants, attributes include hourly rate (for calculation of the budget), commission, expertise and curriculum data. The leaveDate field records when a consultant leaves the company, (the field should be null before he leaves). In what concerns the participation of a consultant in a task, we record his start and end date in the task, the planned MM that he was expected to work in the task, and the actual MM he worked in the task.

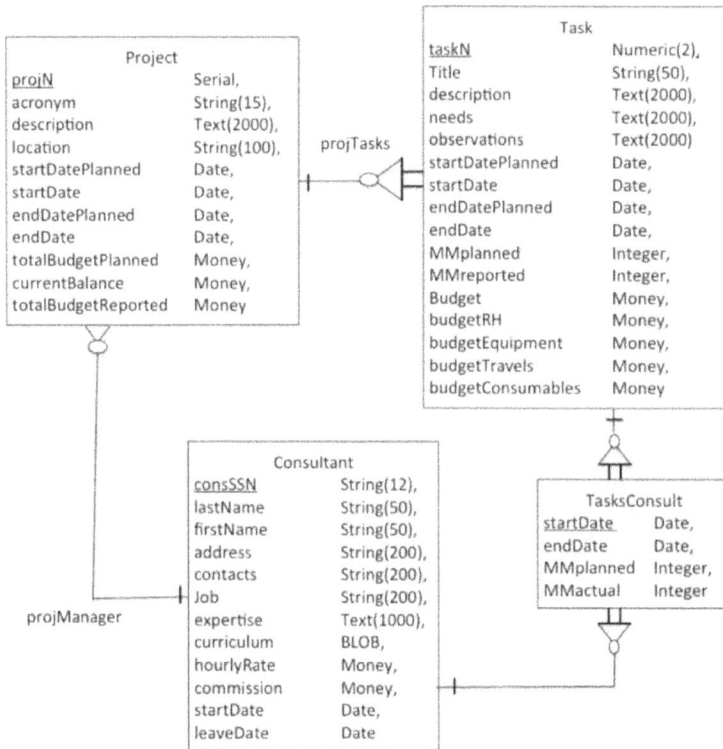

Figure 34. Project-Task-Consultant part of the Projects Database ER

Besides specifying the attributes and their data types, it is important for the designer to document constraints on those attributes, defining the domain and further restrictions as accurately as possible. For instance, we can indicate that an endDate must always be later or equal to the corresponding startDate, or that some attribute of type money must have values between 0 and some upper limit.

Summarizing the whole process that we described in this chapter, the designer should start by describing the real-world problem and the requirements. Then he should start working on a first draft of the ER diagram, representing entities, relationships and identifiers. Then, it is a good idea to use computerized tools to draw a complete version of the ER diagram, adding attributes, domains, constraints and all other relevant information. The relational diagram is generated automatically by the tool, using a set of rules of transformation executed by the machine, without further interaction from the designer. But if no tool is available, the designer can also generate the relational diagram manually, by applying transformation rules.

It is important for the designer to know the transformation rules, the rules that transform an ER into a relational schema, to better understand how he should design the ER model and the consequences of his design choices in terms of generated relational model, and to make choices regarding generation options. One example of a choice is how to materialize an inheritance relationship. The next chapter describes the rules and important knowledge that the designer needs to have concerning the translation from ER model to relational model.

6. Entity-Relationship to Relational

The process of translation of the Entity-Relationship (ER) diagram into a Relational (R) diagram is based on a set of rules. Some of the rules are exclusively related to transformation of entities and relationships into relations (conceptual model into physical model), while other rules can also be applied to transform the representation within the Entity-Relationship model (conceptual to conceptual).

The rules are logical consequences of the meanings of entities, relationships and constraints, and how they should be represented in a relational model. We present each rule, followed by a discussion. The discussion reviews the rationale of the rules, how you should think when applying the rules, and how you should think about exceptions, cases where you may decide not to apply the rule.

If non-null referential constraints are relaxed to allow null references, the rules become much simpler. We advocate such simplification, therefore we conclude the discussion of each rule with a simplified version of the rule (Simplified Rule), which can be applied instead of the more elaborate version. Finally, we provide examples for each rule.

6.1. R(e). Entity-to-Relation Default Transformation

By default, and entity is transformed into a relation. Exceptions are consequence of what is stated in other rules. When an entity is transformed into a relation, the identifier of the entity becomes the primary key of the relation.

Discussion - entities of the ER model usually give rise to relations in the Relational Model. However, entities are a more abstract concept than relations and, depending on the transformation rule that is applied, may not translate into relations. For instance, two entities and a relationship can merge into a single relation, or an inheritance with one parent and three children can be transformed into one, two, three or four relations.

6.2. R(1:1). Transformations of 1:1 Relationships

Mandatory participations on both sides of the relationship – two entities with one-to-one relationships with mandatory participation on both sides are transformed into a single entity (conceptual-conceptual) or a single relation (conceptual-physical), whose identifier/primary key can be the identifier/primary key of any of the two entities. The name of the resulting entity/relation can be the concatenation of the names of both entities.

Mandatory participation on one side of the relationship – two entities with one-to-one relationship with mandatory participation on one side and optional on the other side are transformed into two relations, one corresponding to each entity, and the primary key of each corresponds to the identifier of the corresponding entity. The relation corresponding to the entity with mandatory participation in the relationship will have a foreign key referencing the other relation. The foreign key references the primary key of the other relation.

Optional participation on both sides of the relationship – two entities with one-to-one relationship with optional participation on both sides are transformed into three relations, one corresponding to each entity, and a third representing the relationship. The relation representing the relationship will have as foreign keys the identifier of each entity. The primary key of the relationship relation will be one of the identifiers of one of the entities.

Simplification - A variation of this last case of optional participation on both sides is to always transform into two relations, one corresponding to each entity. One of the two relations will have a foreign key referencing the other relation (the foreign key references the identifier of the other relation). This alternative saves one relation (the relationship relation), in exchange of allowing the foreign key to take null values.

Discussion - In 1:1 mandatory relationships, for one instance of one of the entities, there is a single instance of the other entity that relates to it. Fusing the two entities into one is easy, since instances of the resulting entity are simply putting together the instances that relate to each other as a single larger instance.

When one side of the relationship has optional participation, if we fuse the two entities into a single relation, the optionality means that some tuples of the fused relation end up with all attributes of the optional side being null (this may even be forbidden if some attribute(s) has a non-null constraint). This is why the rule does not fuse both entities together in this case. The relationship is instead represented by the foreign key, and the foreign key is placed in the relation with mandatory participation, because this ensures that it will not be null.

In this scenario of 1:1 with optional participation on both sides, the transformation rule demands transformation into three relations, one being the relationship relation. The reason for this is because otherwise there would need to be a foreign key in one of the two relations, and that foreign key could take the value null for some tuples. This is a consequence of participation being optional.

This transformation rule for optionality on both sides demanding transformation into three relations is often replaced by the more sensible solution that avoids the need for three relations. If we allow null values in the foreign key attribute, we can have only two relations to represent the scenario 1:1 with optionality on both sides. A foreign key is added to one of the two relations referencing the other relation, such that tuples unrelated to any tuple of the other relation will have null as the value for that foreign key. We suggest using this relaxed variation of the rule, since it reduces complexity. The most simplified version of the rule is:

Simplified 1:1 Rule - 1:1 relationships are transformed into two relations, one for each entity, where the primary key of each relation is the identifier of the corresponding entity, and each relation has a foreign key that references the primary key of the other relation.

Example – One-to-one relationships are most frequently associated with a well-defined "subject" that is composed by a set of attributes and can be associated as part of the other entity, but can also be considered an entity itself. In the example, a Customer has an Address. The Address is a well-defined "subject" itself, with a set of attributes that includes the country, city, street, door number. A customer has an address, and in Figure 35(a) the customer must always be associated with an address, and an address must always be associated with one and a single customer. Representing the customer and address as two separate entities in this example is an option, there is no need to have the two entities. We could have included the address attributes directly as part of the customer entity.

Figure 35(b) shows the relation that results from applying rule R(1:1) to the ER model of Figure 35(a). It is a single relation with all the attributes of both customer and address, and the primary key of the relation is the primary key of the customer. We could instead materialize Figure 35(a) into two relations, one for each entity, but in this particular example, and considering only the information that is in Figure 35(a), the relational model of Figure 35(b) seems adequate. Both the ER and the relational models could be represented as a single entity.

In Figure 36(a) we show a slightly different case. In this case the customer may have an address associated with her/him or not, and this is represented as an optional participation of entity Customer in the relationship.

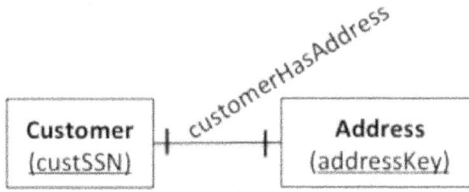

(a) Customer-Address: entities and relationships (ER)

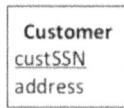

(b) Customer-Address: relation (R)

Figure 35. Customer-Address (Mandatory) Example

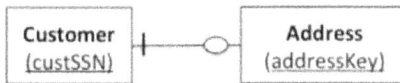

(a) Customer-Address: entities and relationships (ER)

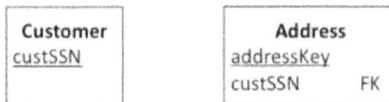

(b) Customer-Address: relations option 1 (R)

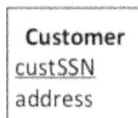

(c) Customer-Address: relations option 2 (R)

Figure 36.Customer-Address (Optional) Example

Since the participation is optional, if we follow the strict version of rule R(1:1), we should have the two relations of Figure 36(b). Each entity is transformed into a relation, and the Address relation has a foreign key referencing the customer. Since an address must always be associated with a customer, the foreign key is always filled with some non-null value.

In Figure 36(c) we show the alternative of including the address attributes in the customer relation. In this case, when a customer has no address associated with her/him, the Address attributes (country, city, street, door number) will be unfilled, which is represented by null values. This can be more error prone than Figure 36(b), since the non-existence of an address for a customer results in a set of null attributes.

6.3. R(1:N). Transformations of 1:N Relationships

1:N Mandatory on the :N side – the entities are transformed into two relations, one for each entity, and the relation on the :N side will have a foreign key attribute referencing the primary identifier of the other relation.

1:N Optional on the :N side - the entities are transformed into three relations, one for each entity and one for the relationship. The relationship relation will have as foreign keys the identifiers of the other two relations, and the primary key of the relationship relation will be the primary identifier of the relation on the :N side.

Simplification - The alternative transformation rule, assuming that foreign keys can hold null values, is to transform the entities into two relations, where the :N side relation will have a foreign key that references the primary identifier of the 1: side relation. This foreign key can have null values (when there is no related 1: instance).

Discussion - In One-to-Many relationships, one instance of one entity may be related with multiple instances of the other relation. If we were to have a foreign key in the 1: side, referencing all related instances in the N side, the foreign key attribute would have to be multi-valued, to hold the set of referenced instances. However, we are not allowed to have multi-valued attributes in the relational model. The rules for 1:N relationships are a simple work-around for this limitation. Since the foreign key is placed in the N: side of the relationship, it only references one instance of the other entity (N:1), which avoids multi-valued attributes.

Simplified 1:N Rule - 1:N relationships are always transformed into two relations, one for each entity, where the primary key of each relation is the identifier of the corresponding entity, and the relation corresponding to the N: side has a foreign key that references the primary key of the other relation (the foreign key may have null value when there is no associated instance of the other relation).

Example – In Figure 37(a) a project can have multiple tasks, and a task is associated with one and only one project. According to rule R(1:N), this results in a relational model shown in Figure 37(b), where Task has a foreign key referencing entity Project.

We already mentioned and will discuss further later on that the Project-Task relationship would be much better represented as a weak relationship, Task being a dependent entity on Project. This is because a task does not exist without a project and the project is part of the identification of the task in the relational model.

(a)   Project-Task: entities and relationships (ER)

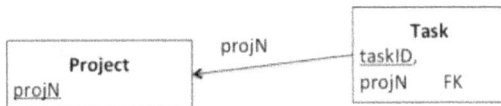

(b)   Project-Task: Relational (R)

Figure 37. Project-Task 1:N Relationship

According to the same rule, if the participation of Task in the relationship was also optional (a task could exist even without being associated with any project), the entity-relationship diagram would be similar to that of Figure 38(a). In this case, the strict version of rule R(1:N) would require you to create three relations (Project, ProjectTask and Task) to represent the relational model, as shown in Figure 38(b). However, you can apply the simplified version of the rule to have Figure 38(c). This representation is much simpler to use, and the only extra assumption you need to make is that the foreign key projN in task can have null values to represent tasks that would not be associated with any project.

(a)   Project-Task II: entities and relationships (ER)

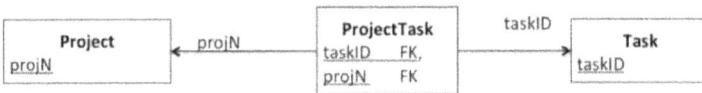

(b)   Project-Task II: Relational option 1 (R)

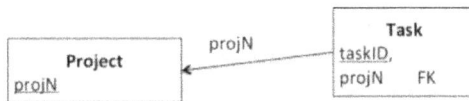

(c)   Project-Task II: Relational option 2 (R)

Figure 38. Project-Task 1:N Optional Relationship

6.4. R(N:M). Transformations of N:M Relationships

N:M Relationships – Many-to-Many relationships always give rise to three relations, one for each entity and one for representing the relationship. The relation representing the relationship will have as foreign keys attributes referencing the identifiers of the two entities, and the both foreign key attributes are also part of the primary key of the relation.

N:M Relationships, conceptual transformation – An M:N relationship can be transformed into a weak entity with dependent relationships to each of the original entities.

Discussion - Given that each instance of both entities relates to multiple instances of the other entity, if we would try to keep only two relations, the foreign key of each referencing the other relation would have multi-valued attributes, which is not possible in the relational model. Therefore, we need to have a relation representing the relationship, which indicates which instances of one entity are related to which instances of the other by means of pairs of identifier values.

The second part of the rule, concerning conceptual transformation, is a way to transform the M:N relationships into two 1:N relationships between a new entity, representing the relationship, and the two original entities. The relationship entity indicates which instances of one entity relate to which instances of the other entity.

Example – The Supplier-Product ER diagram shown in Figure 39(a) represents suppliers of products, where one supplier can supply multiple products and a product can be supplied by multiple suppliers. Following the rule R(M:N), we will end up with three relations, Product, Supplier and Supply. The Supply relation represents the relationship, and is composed of pairs supplierID and productID. It indicates who supplies which product.

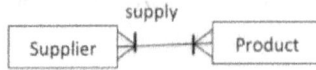

(a) Supplier-Product: entity-relationship (ER)

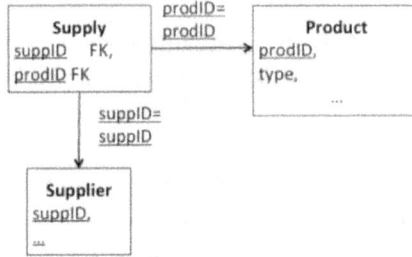

(b) Supplier-Product: Relational (R)

Figure 39. Supplier-Product M:N Example

6.5. Rweak. Weak 1:N (and 1:1) Relationships

A weak 1:N (and 1:1) relationship has two entities: the parent entity and the dependent (a.k.a. weak) entity. The dependent entity is dependent of the parent entity, which means that its existence is dependent of the parent, and its identity is partly defined by the identity of the parent. The dependent entity is transformed into a "dependent" relation, whose primary key will include the primary identifier of the parent entity, and that primary key part referencing the parent entity will also be foreign key to the parent relation.

Example – A task is part of a project, and a project has multiple tasks. For a task to be defined, it must be in the context of a project, and the task is identified as task number X in project Py. A task is dependent on the project it belongs to. It does not exist without the project, and it is partly identified as part of the project. Therefore, the entity Task can best be described as an entity that is dependent on the Project entity. Figure 40(a) shows the representation of such dependency. Figure 40(b) shows the corresponding relational diagram, according to rule Rweak. In that diagram we can see that the primary key of Task includes projN, which is also the reference to the parent relation Project. Task is also identified by the task number taskN, therefore it is defined by the project and the task number.

(a) Project-Task II: entity-relationship (ER)

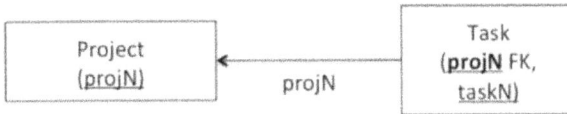

(b) Project-Task II: relational (R)

Figure 40. Project-Task II: Dependent Entity and Relationship

We have defined the Project-Task relationship before in Figure 37 as a non-dependent 1:N relationship. In particular, Figure 37(a) and Figure 40(a) are quite similar, the difference being the use of the dependent relationship symbol. The corresponding relational diagrams of Figure 37(b) and Figure 40(b) have subtle differences. First of all, the primary key of Task in Figure 37(b) is only made of attribute taskID, therefore the task is identified by a single attribute that is not referencing the project. For instance, we could have a task identified as taskID=PyT1. We also have a foreign key to the project in that diagram, but that foreign key is not part of the primary key of Task. We could for instance make the mistake of calling PzT1 to a task of project Py. The representation of Figure 40(b) is simpler and more direct, since the project identifier is part of the primary key of the task itself (due to the dependency). In that case, task Tx of project Py is identified simply as having projN=Py, which is simultaneously the reference to the Project tuple of project Py, and task number taskN=Tx. This is the advantage of representing and using dependent relationships in the ER model when they should be used instead of ordinary relationships.

On the other hand, in certain cases, representing all dependent entities as such can lead to long primary keys, in which case we may resort to having some entities as dependent, while others will be represented as ordinary relationships.

6.6. RI. Inheritance Relationships

In inheritance relationships, there is a parent entity (P) and children entities (C_i). A child is of the same type of the parent, but is also a sub-type with specific properties, relationships or both. The parent entity should hold all attributes that are common to all children, and the children entities should hold their own specific attributes (attributes that they do not share with the other children), exclusively. It is also a good design choice to include a type attribute in the parent entity, which indicates the type of children that a particular instance belongs to.

Depending on what is the best design choice, we can decide to materialize as relations only a single relation that includes all attributes from all entities (represented here as P+C_i), only children relations (C_i), both parent and children relations (P and C_i) or parent and some children (P and some C_i). Next we discuss those alternatives and the rationale that leads to choosing one of them.

RI1. Only parent (P+C_i): there will be a single relation that contains all parent attributes and all attributes of all children as well. This is the most logical option when children have no attributes and no relationships with any other entities. If this is not the case, this alternative may still be the logical choice if the number of attributes/relationships of children are few.

As an example, the Customer example of Figure 41 would be transformed into the relation of Figure 42.

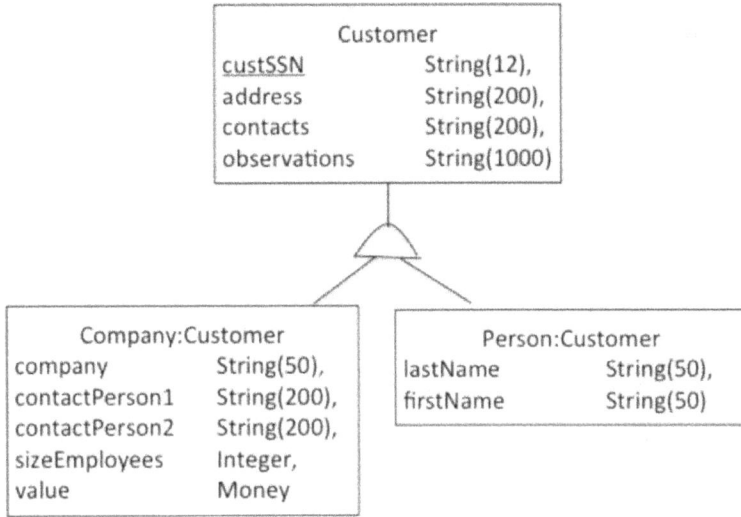

Figure 41. Customer and its Inheritance Relationship

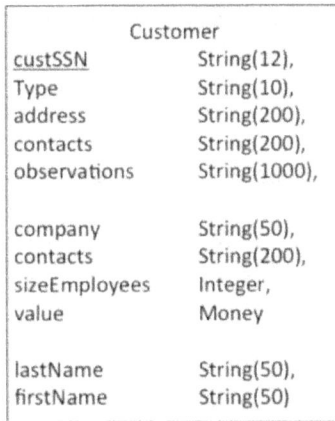

Figure 42. Customer Inheritance (P+C$_i$)

This could probably not be considered a good choice for the example of Customer, since companies and individual customers both have several specific attributes that will be left unfilled when the customer has the other type. Using this alternative, customers Jorge Silva (individual) and CompanyX (company) would be represented as the following tuples (notice the null company fields for customer Jorge Silva, and the null

Person fields for CompanyX),

Customer(
//custSSN, type,   address, contacts, observations
203456765, 'Person','Rua da Alegria, 216, Lisboa, Portugal','21-223543, 96-3454332', null,

  //company,   contactPerson1, contactPerson2 , sizeEmployees, value
  null,null,null,null,null,

  //lastName, firstName
  'Jorge', 'Silva'
)

Customer(
//custSSN, type,   address, contacts, observations
103355769, 'Company', 'Expo, 216, Lisboa, Portugal','21-129533, 21-2674322', null,

  //company,   contactPerson1, contactPerson2 , sizeEmployees, value
  'CompanyX','Pedro Mexia','Manuel Brinca',7000,2000000,

  //lastName, firstName
  null, null
)

RI2. Only children (C_i): there will be one relation for each children of the inheritance relationship, and no relation for the parent. Each child relation will have all attributes of the parent entity, plus the attributes of the specific child entity that it represents.

Figure 43 shows the materialization of Customer using this alternative, relations Company and Person.

Company	
custSSN	String(12),
Type	String(10),
address	String(200),
contacts	String(200),
observations	String(1000),
company	String(50),
contacts	String(200),
sizeEmployees	Integer,
value	Money

Person	
custSSN	String(12),
Type	String(10),
address	String(200),
contacts	String(200),
observations	String(1000),
lastName	String(50),
firstName	String(50)

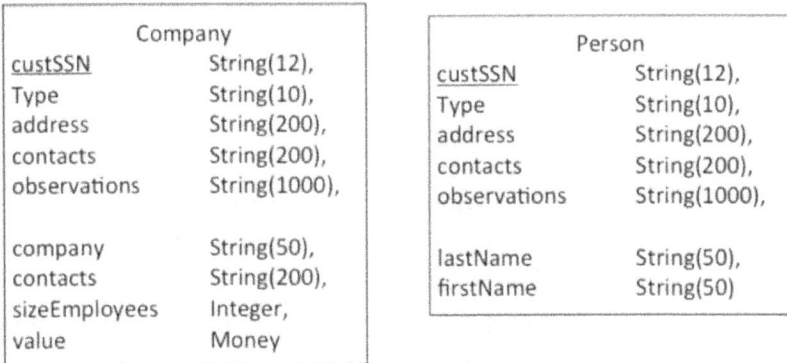

Figure 43. Customer inheritance (C$_i$)

Person(
//custSSN, type, address, contacts, observations
203456765, 'Person','Rua da Alegria, 216, Lisboa, Portugal','21-223543, 96-3454332', null,

   //lastName, firstName
   'Jorge', 'Silva'
)

Company(
//custSSN, type, address, contacts, observations
103355769, 'Company', 'Expo, 216, Lisboa, Portugal','21-129533, 21-2674322', null,

   //company,   contactPerson1, contactPerson2 , sizeEmployees, value
   'CompanyX','Pedro Mexia','Manuel Brinca',7000,2000000,
)

RI3. Parent and children relations (P and C$_i$): one relation is created representing the parent entity, and one more relation per child is created for representing each child. The parent keeps the attributes that are common to all children and the identifier, while each child keeps the attributes that are specific to it, plus the identifier of the entity. The identifier is used as primary key in all relations (parent and children), and it is also a foreign key in each children, referencing the identifier of the parent relation.

This alternative represents a tuple of a customer as two actual tuples, one will be in the parent relation and the other one in the child. Figure 44 shows the result of materializing the Customer entity using this approach. Each relation keeps the attributes of the corresponding entity, and the children relations receive the custSSN attribute that is used to identify the customer and to link to the rest of the information of the same customer in the parent relation.

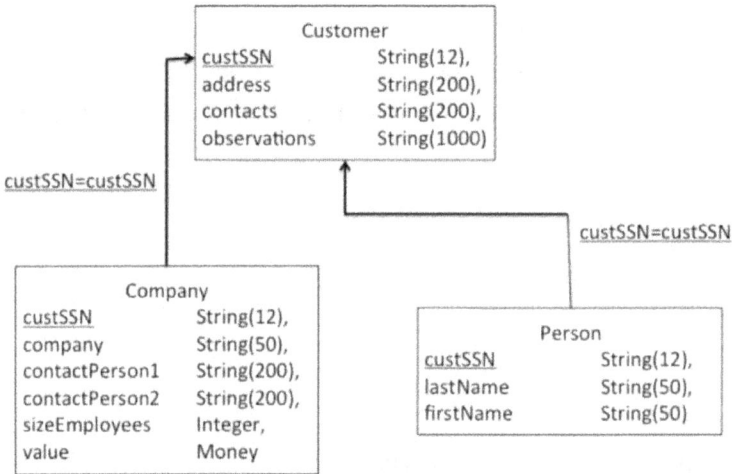

Figure 44. Relational Model of alternative (P and C$_i$)

Insertions/deletions of costumers require insertion/deletion in two relations (the parent and the child). Next we show the tuples that represent an individual and a company:

Customer tuple 1(
//custSSN, type,   address, contacts, observations
203456765, 'Person','Rua da Alegria, 216, Lisboa, Portugal','21-223543, 96-3454332', null)

Customer2 tuple 2(
//custSSN, type,   address, contacts, observations
//custSSN, type,   address, contacts, observations
103355769, 'Company', 'Expo, 216, Lisboa, Portugal','21-129533, 21-2674322', null,
)

Person(
  //custSSN,lastName, firstName
  203456765, 'Jorge', 'Silva'
)

Company(
  //custSSN,company,   contactPerson1,   contactPerson2   ,
sizeEmployees,   value
  103355769   'CompanyX','Pedro   Mexia','Manuel
Brinca',7000,2000000,
)

In order to see information of customers who are individuals, we need to issue the SQL command that joins both relations Customer and Person,

Select customer.custSSN, address, contacts, observations, lastName, firstName
From Person, Customer
Where Person.custSSN=Customer.custSSN;

As a curiosity, we could also formulate the transformation rule of the (P and C_i) alternative at the level of the Entity-Relationship model (conceptual-conceptual) . The entities would be transformed such that the inheritance relationship would be replaced by a 1:1 dependent (a.k.a weak) relationship of each child to the parent, as shown in Figure 45 for the Customer example. If we next transform this model into a relational model following the rule for dependent relationships (RWeak), we will get the result shown in Figure 44.

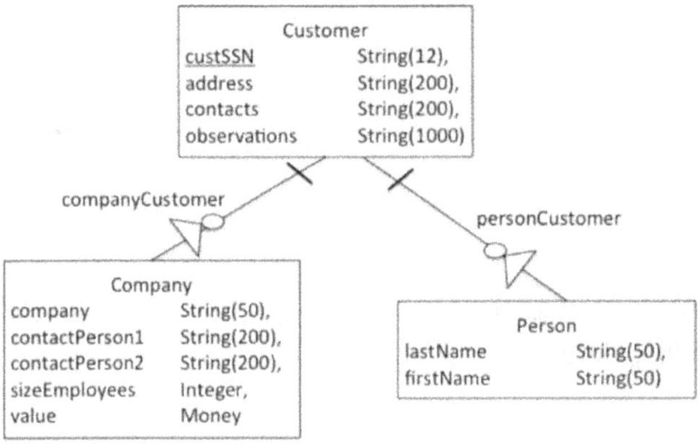

Figure 45. (P and C$_i$) Conceptual-to-conceptual Transformation

RI4. Parent and some children (P and some C$_i$): Some children are transformed using alternative I1, the remaining use the approach in I3. This is used for instance when some of the children have few or no attributes, therefore they can be represented using the parent without too many null values.

Figure 46 is an example relational model of the (P and some C$_i$) alternative for the Customer entity.

Rule RI4 (Parent and some children) is the rule that we would suggest as most adequate for most cases. It keeps a parent relation where you can search irrespective of the type of children, avoids having too many null attributes (which can happen when you apply RI1), and it still allows the designer to consider not materializing some child entity. On the down side, it requires dealing with two relations when doing some operations such as insert of tuples of a single entity instance. This would not be needed if you would use RI1 or RI2.

```
                              ┌──────────────────────────────────────────┐
                              │            Customer                        │
                        ┌────→│  custSSN          String(12),              │
                        │     │  address          String(200),             │
                        │     │  contacts          String(200),            │
                        │     │  observations     String(1000)             │
                        │     │  lastName         String(50),              │
   custSSN=custSSN      │     │  firstName        String(50)               │
                        │     └──────────────────────────────────────────┘
                        │
       ┌────────────────┴───────────────────┐
       │            Company                  │
       │  custSSN          String(12),       │
       │  company          String(50),       │
       │  contactPerson1   String(200),      │
       │  contactPerson2   String(200),      │
       │  sizeEmployees    Integer,          │
       │  value            Money             │
       └─────────────────────────────────────┘
```

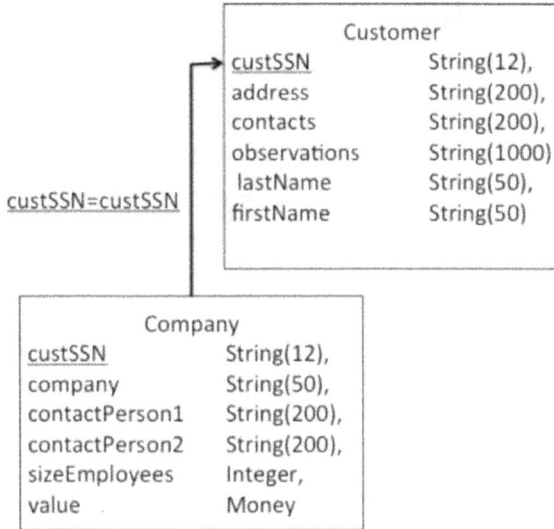

Figure 46. Relational Model of alternative (P and some C$_i$)

6.7. Complete ER-R Transformation Examples

In this section we apply the rules that we described in the previous section to the database projects that we have been using as examples. As we proceed, we also discuss some additional details that are useful to simplify and make the design clearer.

6.7.1. Example 1. Projects Database

In Figure 47 we show the relational model that results from applying ER-R transformation rules to the Projects database example. Only primary key and foreign key attributes are shown, for the sake of clarity. The remaining attributes, shown in Figure 32, Figure 33 and Figure 34 can be added. We also indicate the rule that determined each transformation.

In the figure, primary key attributes are underlined, foreign key attributes are in bold and also include the FK keyword in front of them, and some of the attributes are both primary keys and foreign keys, in which case they are underlined, in bold and have the keyword FK in front.

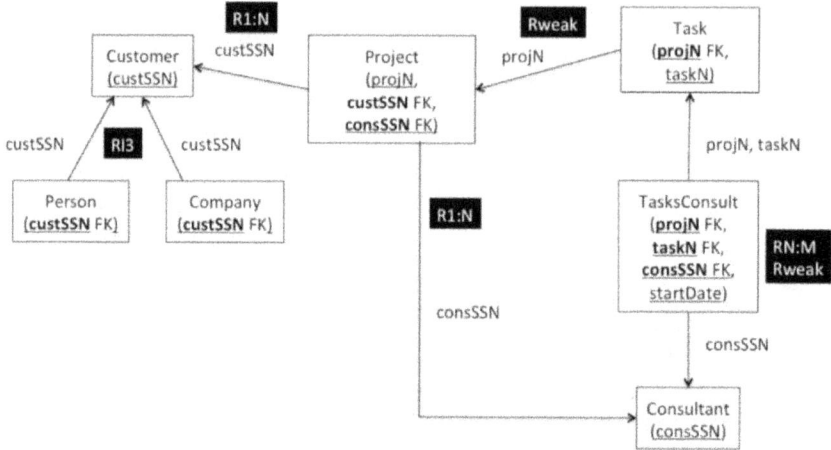

Figure 47. Relational Model of the Projects Database

In this example we used the same names for foreign keys as the corresponding names of the attributes in the referenced relation. In fact, there is no need to do so. Just to show that this is not mandatory, in Figure 48 we replaced the names of the foreign keys of relation Project that reference the customer and the consultant with suggestive names (customer and consultant). Notice that the referencing links between relations in the figure indicate which attributes are doing the link (custSSN=customer and consSSN=consultant).

The TaskConsult relation has a quite big primary key, made of many (4) attributes. The size of that primary key is a consequence of it receiving primary key parts from other entities (Task and Consultant) due to being dependent on them, besides its own part of the key (startDate), and of Task itself being dependent of Project. We always have a choice to create an artificial primary key instead of using natural primary keys. In this case this option means that we can decide to replace the huge primary key by a single attribute, which is an artificial key that we add to the design. If we do so, the 4 attributes that are currently the primary key will still be there, and 3 of them will still be foreign keys, the only difference is that the primary key will be the new attribute. The new attribute, which we called taskConsultID, should be a serial (sequence) attribute that gets incremental values automatically.

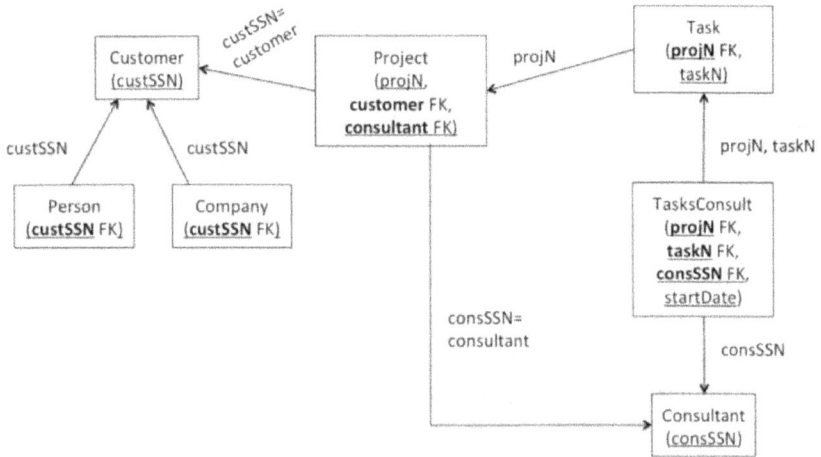

Figure 48. Refined Relational Model of the Projects Database

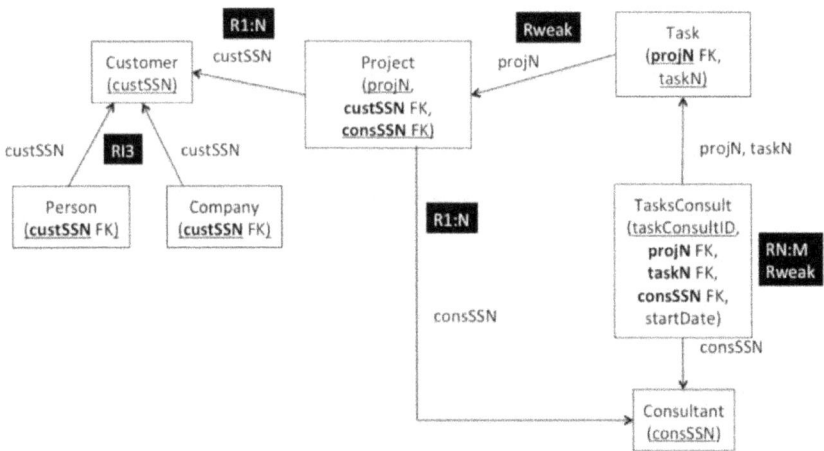

Figure 49. Refined Relational Model of the Projects Database

The schema of the Projects database has the following attributes in each relation:

Customer(custSSN, type, address , contacts, observations);
Company (custSSN FK, company, contactPerson1,

contactPerson2, sizeEmployees, value);
Person(lastName, firstName);

Project(projN, custSSN FK, consSSN FK, acronym, description, location,
startDateplanned, startDate, endDateplanned, endDate,
totalBudgetplanned, currentBalance, totalBudgetreported
)

Task(projN, taskN, title, description, needs, observations,
startDateplanned, startDate, endDateplanned, endDate,
mmplanned, mmreported,
budget, budgetRH, budgetEquipment, budgetConsumables
)

Consultant(consSSN,
lastName, firstName, address, contacts,
            Job, expertise, curriculum,
hourlyRate, commission,
startDate, leaveDate
)

TaskConsultant(projN FK, taskN FK, consSSN FK, startDate,
numberOfDays, description)

The following CREATE TABLE statements are used to create this schema in a target database (these are pseudo-code statements that you may nee to modify slightly depending on the database engine where they will run):

CREATE TABLE Customer(
custSSN PRIMARY KEYNumeric(10),
type   Varchar(15),
address   Varchar(1000),
contacts   Varchar(200),
observations   Varchar(2000)
);

```
CREATE TABLE Company (
custSSN PRIMARY KEYNumeric(10),
company        Varchar(100),
contactPerson1   Varchar(100),
contactPerson2   Varchar(100),
sizeEmployees   Numeric(6),
value          Numeric(10),
FOREIGN KEY custSSN references Customer(custSSN)
);


CREATE TABLE Person(
custSSN PRIMARY KEYNumeric(10),
lastName       Varchar(100),
firstName      Varchar(100),
FOREIGN KEY custSSN references Customer(custSSN)
);


CREATE TABLE Project(
projN PRIMARY KEYSerial,
customer       Numeric(10)
REFERENCES Customer(custSSN),
projectManager   Numeric(10)
REFERENCES Consultant(consSSN),
Acronym        Varchar(100),
Description    Varchar(1000),
Location       Varchar(100),
startDatePlanned   Date,
startDate      Date
endDatePlanned   Date
endDate        Date
 CHECK(endDate>startDate),
totalBudgetplannedNumeric(10,2),
currentBalance   Numeric(10,2),
totalBudgetreported Numeric(10,2)
);
```

```
CREATE TABLE Task(
projN              PRIMARY KEY Numeric(10),
taskN              PRIMARY KEY Numeric(10),
title              NOT NULLVarchar(100),
description        Varchar(1000),
needs              Varchar(1000),
observations       Varchar(2000),
startDatePlanned   Date,
startDate          Date
endDatePlanned     Date
endDate            Date
 CHECK(endDate>startDate),
MMplanned          Numeric(5),
MMreported         Numeric(5),
budget             Numeric(10,2),
budgetRH           Numeric(10,2),
budgetEquipment    Numeric(10,2),
budgetConsumablesNumeric(10,2)
);

CREATE TABLE Consultant(
consSSN     PRIMARY KEYNumeric(10),
lastName    NOT NULLVarchar(100),
firstName   NOT NULLVarchar(100),
address            Varchar(1000),
contacts           Varchar(100),
job                Varchar(100),
expertise          Varchar(100),
curriculum         BLOB,
hourlyRate         Numeric(5,2),
commission         Numeric(5,2),
startDate          Date,
leaveDate          Date
);
```

```
CREATE TABLE TaskConsultant(
projN           PRIMARY KEY Numeric(10),
taskN           PRIMARY KEY Numeric(10),
consSSN         PRIMARY KEY Numeric(10),
startDate       PRIMARY KEY Numeric(10),
numberOfDays    Numeric(10),
description     Varchar(1000),
FOREIGN KEY projN REFERENCES Task(projN),
FOREIGN KEY taskN REFERENCES Task(taskN),
FOREIGN KEY consSSN REFERENCES Consultant(consSSN)
);
```

6.7.2. Example 2. Relational Food Quality Database

Figure 50 shows the relational model for the food quality control database. This model was derived from the ER model of Figure 24. It is the result of applying the ER-R transformation rules that were defined in this chapter. Product Type records the types of products handled in the factory, while Product Unit stores each individual package and container of products, with a serial number that identifies the product unit uniquely. We know which products go into which batches by means of the identification of the batch that is stored in the 'Product Unit' relation. The relation 'Production' keeps track of what batches of raw products were used in the production of what batches of output products, based on the batchNum foreign keys. This relational model should be completed with the remaining attributes of interest, and the SQL/DDL. Those tasks are left to the reader as an exercise.

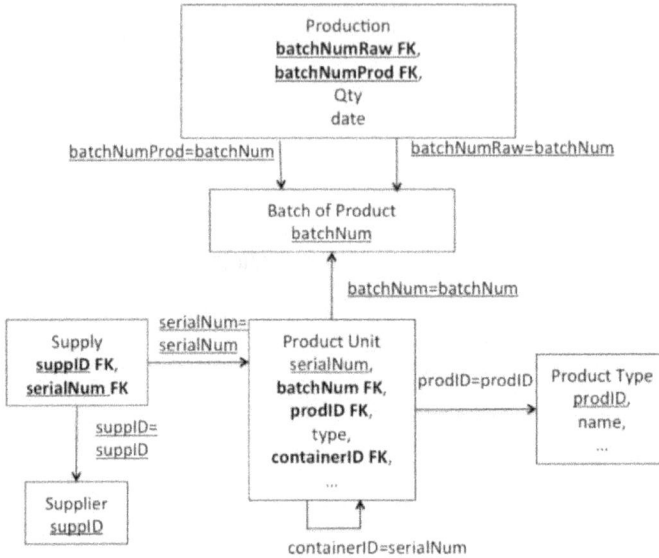

Figure 50. Relational Model for Food Quality Control Database

6.7.3.Example 3. Relational Model of Clinical Information

The ER diagram for the Clinical Information Database was shown in Figure 25. In order to take decisions, we would need to study the attributes required for each entity, but since we are focusing on the transformations between ER and relational models, we make some simple assumptions instead of looking at all the detail. Concerning the "Hospital Clinical Staff", we will consider that Nurses and Technicians can be represented exclusively in the entity "Hospital Clinical Staff", while Medical Doctors need to be represented separately, due to a number of specific attributes and relationships that other clinical staff do not need to store. In what concerns exams, we consider that the symptoms and diagnosis can be lengthy text attributes, and that observations and conclusions of exams are described in an attribute "observation". The only exam types that require additional information are imaging and bio analysis exams. In those cases, we need to store images and their observation data, and numeric or BLOB data in what concerns bio analysis exams. The Bio Indicators entity will also store information concerning normal intervals of those indicators.

Figure 51 shows the relational model after we have applied the transformation rules studied in this chapter. As an exercise to better understand how this schema works, the reader can try to insert data about hospital visits, clinical episodes and exams of different types. Another exercise is to think about the attributes that each entity and each table should have. Some missing attributes are quite obvious, for instance, the date and time when one exam was made, as well as dates and times for hospital visits and when a clinical episode was recorded.

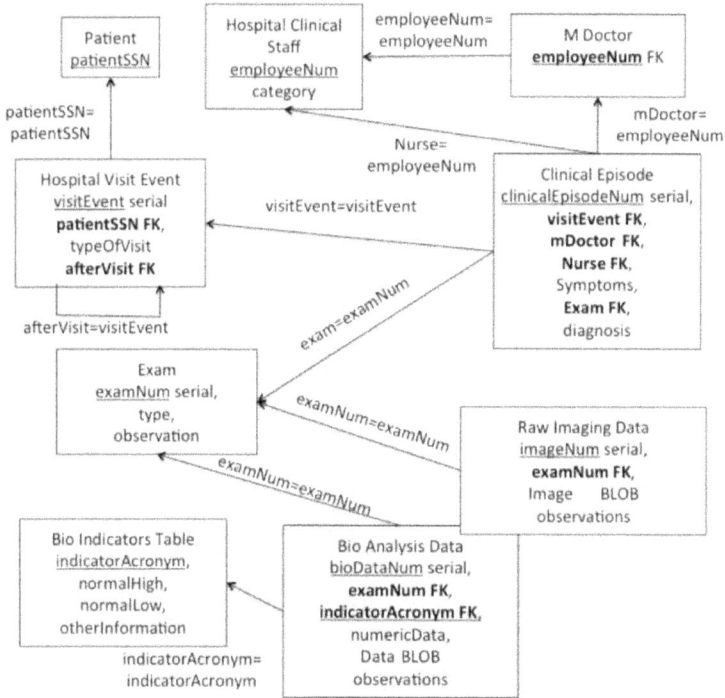

Figure 51. Relational Model for the Clinical Information Database

7. Design and Development

In the previous chapters we have studied how to generate the data schema for database applications, and how to create the corresponding relations (tables) in relational databases. In this chapter we explain the remaining steps and mechanisms for creating applications that handle data. The emphasis is not in particular programming frameworks, since there are many different options and an almost constant evolution. Instead, we focus on explaining the basics of how to design and develop applications, how to connect to the database and how to program database interaction and user interfaces, all of those using de facto standard APIs, languages and approaches. Given this knowledge, the reader is encouraged to further explore specific tools.

7.1. Phases and Paradigm for Design and Development

The process of designing and developing data applications goes through a set of steps typical of Software Engineering (SE) processes. Instead of describing some SE methodology, we focus on a set of important concepts and guidelines the developer should have in mind while designing and developing data applications. Readers particularly interested in the related subject of SE methodologies are encouraged to search for bibliography on Software Engineering Methodologies.

Roughly, the design and development process should include the following concerns:

Requirements analysis – the needs of the application or module to be developed are studied and stated in some systematic, organized manner;

Design – a designer perspective is adopted, in which it is necessary to determine how the application or module will be. This includes user interfaces, data schema, the infrastructure and other aspects of relevance. A high-level design should be independent of the specific technologies that will be used, such as programming language or database engine;

Detailed design – the design is detailed and there is a more exhaustive coverage of the functionality. Detailed design can be or not be dependent of specific technologies, such as programming languages and database engines that will be used. A detailed design is just a continuation of the design, it may or may not exist;

Development or implementation – Given a design, development is concerned with actually coding the application in target languages, database engines or complete frameworks that may be used to produce the application;

Testing – testing is a companion to development. The objective is to certify that the code does what it is intended to do and in an appropriate manner. Test plans can be created and evolved during requirements elicitation, design and detailed design. We do not discuss testing further in this book, since it is out of scope, instead we encourage readers interested in the subject to search for the extensive bibliography on the issue.

Maintenance – applications have a lifetime during which they have to be maintained, sometimes evolved, and even when they become obsolete, they have to be replaced by some new application using more up-to-date technologies. In the case of data applications, data has to be rescued and migrated when system migration happens.

When discussing Design and Development (D&D), it is important to note that historically, the thinking has evolved around two generic paradigms that we organize as: **(a)** Waterfall-based (W-D&D), where design and development is a completely sequential process, with analysis and design of the information system or parts of it being completed before starting any implementation; **(b)** a Module and Spiral-based D&D (MS-D&D in our notation), with shorter design and development cycles of parts of the information system (modules), multiple smaller Design and Development cycles with frequent delivery of modules that should be tested, running and use-ready. This paradigm also tries to use feedback from users, and evolution of the modules based on that user feedback. The MS-D&D paradigm is popular in the state-of-the-art design and development methodologies, such as SCRUM [14]. In order to further clarify the issue, next we review some arguments that can be given concerning some potential limitations of W-D&D and advantages of MS-D&D.

W-D&D follows the design and developments phases (requirements, design, detailed design, implementation and testing) in sequence for a whole system or a significant part of it. This approach lacks flexibility that is desirable in many development scenarios, since there is a long period of time before anything starts to be developed and before anything is up and running. A big all-encompassing design frequently results in huge documentation, uncertainty about actual development, bad choices and implementations, given that there is no early and phased output of parts and few feedback during the D&D process. Support by customers is lost along the lengthy W-D&D process, since they do not see anything working for a long time and it is difficult to adapt and modify parts at the end. Most frequently, bad design or development choices are discovered too late, and there is lack of flexibility to change at that point. There is also no prioritizing or early implementation and feedback of functionality and parts.

In a particular W-D&D for a big project that I witnessed, the requirements and design phase took some months, resulted in many hundreds of pages of documentation, with thousands of screenshots and an immense number of ER diagrams. It took a long time to do the design and documentation. The development team had difficulty using such huge documentation, there was no adequate prioritizing and, most importantly, nothing was working after a whole year of project. The sponsors, who were the company administration, dropped their support for the project. The project team was replaced, and the new team focused on an MS-D&D-like methodology, with smaller but visible returns.

MS-D&D starts by listing the functionalities (we denote as modules) that are recognized as needed and can be designed and developed by parts (some functionalities depend on others that should be developed before). Modules are organized as must-haves, should-haves and nice-to-haves. Design and development of modules is prioritized based on importance of the modules, plans for possibly having parts running at certain times, dependencies, and other factors. The list of modules and urgency to develop can change along the project. The plan is reviewed and modified in periodic meetings that should happen weekly, with short daily work planning also happening at the level of smaller module development teams.

7.2. Requirements and Use Cases

At the onset of the development of a project or of some module, developers want to represent what that system or module should be like, and they want stakeholders to understand and to participate in decisions. Requirements and use cases are structured and systematic descriptions of what the system/module should do. One way to thing about requirements and use cases is to start by stating requirements at a high-level, listing the functionalities/modules that the application should have. Then, when developing individual modules, the module is detailed in the form of requirements and/or use-cases for that module.

A simple way to organize requirements may be to write each as a short paragraph (e.g. up to 4 lines of text), and to organize requirements by sections that represent parts of functionality or other classification, with preferably less than ten requirements per part (to be easy to verify if something is missing). For instance, user authorization and managing the user profile may be a section of the requirements in which we describe the login and the operations that should be possible on the profile.

As with requirements, each use case diagram should be small and either high-level, or focused on some module. Figure 52 shows an example use case for the login and profile management of an application. The simplest use cases have actors (the person icon) and use case balloons listing the functionalities that the actors use. We refer the reader to bibliography on use cases and UML (Unified Modeling Language) for detailed information on use cases [15][16].

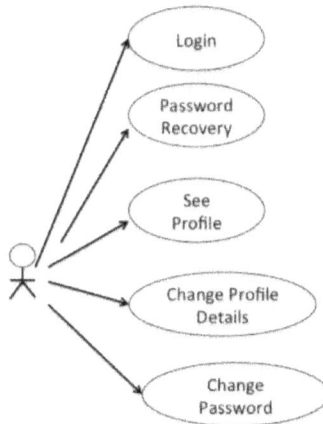

Figure 52. Use Case for Module Login&Profile

7.3. Prototyping and Designing User Interfaces

The objective of UI prototyping (or designing mockups) is to test and describe how some part of the application is expected to work from the perspective of interaction with users, without having to develop any line of code. The simplest prototyping tool is a sheet of paper and a pencil, but there are also computerized applications that allow users to drag and drop components, resize, design the layout and so on.

Since most data applications have a heavy load of interaction with users, mockups are very useful when a team is deciding what should be done and how the application should work and look like. The UI prototype or mockup should be accompanied by a text describing any relevant information that could be of use, and also information on the dynamic aspects of the mockup, e.g., what screen we should see next when we touch some button.

The ATM Login Screen of Figure 53 takes one minute at most to draw, and it conveys some interesting information for the discussion about what should be developed. We can accompany it by a text stating that the code digits are hidden and that, when the last code digit is introduced, the system connects to a central database (which?) and checks against table UserCodes, using variable cardCode read by the card reader and the code userInsertedCode inserted by the user in the keypad. We should also say what happens when the user inserts a wrong code, and so on.

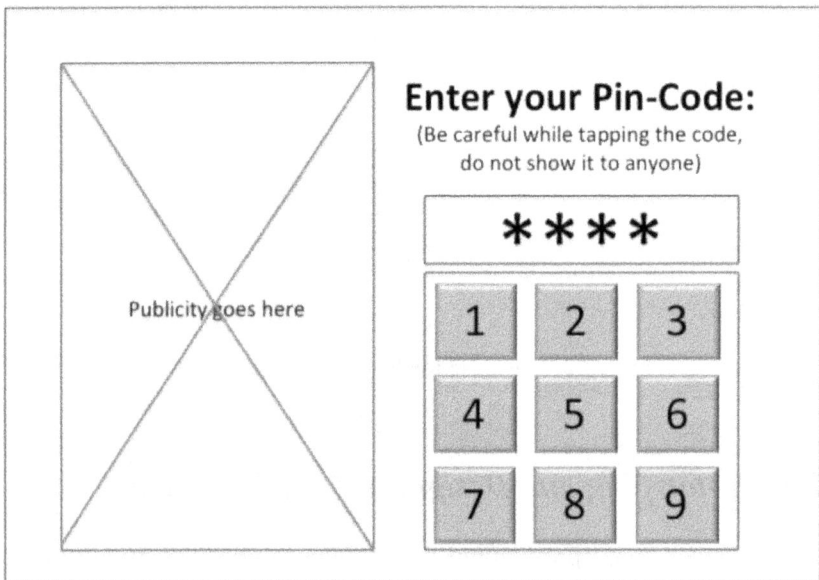

Figure 53. Mockup of ATM Login Screen

The mockup of Figure 53 does not convey information about the flow of screens that is intended in the application, and it may be hard to follow if it has too many screens and dialog boxes. Even if we place all screens in a document, it is probably boring and difficult to follow how the application works, because there may be too many screens. When we are looking at a screen, it conveys no information on the whole picture, only the details of that screen.

One way to show navigation as well as each screen is to have a functional prototype that is coded with the screens, navigation options and menus that actually work. Each screen does not actually have backend logic associated with it except navigation code. This is interesting for validating the application design within the development team, project management team and customers, but it can take precious time to develop.

7.4. Some D&D Guidelines for Small Projects

Simple guidelines can be followed when doing D&D of small or medium data application projects.

One of the first steps is working on the requirements. There should be a small but systematic and well-organized listing of generic requirements, which should include not only functional requirements, but also infrastructure and other requirements. You can organize requirements into sections (e.g. separated by functional parts, and also by types of requirements), and provide numbering (with section.requirement numbering). Use case diagrams may help organizing ideas and defining the relevant parts and uses of the applications.

Given the worries about size and intractability of large projects by human designers and developers, we suggest that the whole project be divided logically and D&D be done by manageable parts, one at a time, or partly in parallel by different coordinated teams working on parts of the project.

You should dimension the project team adequately, try to list what could go wrong (risks) and contingency plans. Some projects will have only yourself, other projects will have a whole team. Plan what documentation the project should have (too much is useless, boring and time wasting, too little or inadequate is risky, but the crucial thing is deciding what the documentation should be).

You should plan the D&D (timings and details) of functional parts and also inside each functional part, so that you plan to have some parts working along the way. Prioritize, label as must, should, nice-to-have. Evolve the plan weekly.

After all the setup, a cyclic set of D&D phases starts. Decide what to D&D in the first phase. Later, repeat the whole process for the other parts.

Design the part. It would be desirable for the part to be reasonably small and for the design to be quick. Design the ER diagram (which can also include entities of other parts, or even the whole project ER). Design only the most important mockups, describe them carefully. Design the menus, buttons, switching behavior between mockups. Review within the development team daily. Review with the project team in review meetings when you stabilized the first version of the design. Improve the design in short cycles, it is desirable that you take at most a week until you are ready to implement a part, or a bit more if the part is larger. Plan tests.

Plan the implementation of the part. Plan a small period for the implementation, perhaps a week, depending on the size of the part. Implement in the planned time frame (the part should be sufficiently small to be implemented in time). Establish rules and best practices to ensure clear and homogenous coding practice, include naming conventions, indentation, non-repetitions (reuse) and so on. Use daily meetings to check the status, take decisions, adapt to changes that may be needed. Inside coding teams, have code reviews with a predefined periodicity, to ensure that good practices are being followed, including also homogenous coding practice of developers. This is a preventive measure to avoid painful debugging of errors later on, and it can also serve to remove undisciplined programmers form the project.

Test, correct, make the code of the part ready for use, have small user manual ready. Make it available and used by users if possible. Collect their feedback, plan for evolution. Go back to the priority list and next parts to be developed.

7.5. Using the Database: Console and Applications

Figure 54 shows a logical diagram with the parts of a data application. The database holds persistent data (Database in the figure) that is managed by the application code (App Code in the figure). The App Code is an executable code that implements Business Logic (operations that the data application needs), and launches user interfaces (User Interfaces or UI in the figure). It is resident in a computerized system, and the UI launched by the App Code interacts with users of the system. In the case of web applications, the user interfaces are web-browsers, the App Code are web-servers, and the Database are databases installed in some database servers.

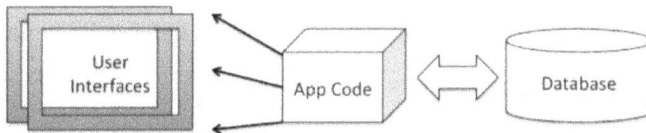

Figure 54. Parts of a Data Application

Each of the three parts depicted in the figure can run remotely, which means that they can run in devices that are physically separated. For example, the database can reside in a server in some place, the App Code can be in another server elsewhere, and it may start a large number of UI instances that will each run on some portable device elsewhere. The UI receives coded instructions and data from the App Code, captures user interactions and data, and submits them back to the App Code. For instance, the UI code may be HTML and Javascript loaded from some App Code, generating web pages in browsers for interaction with users. The UI then receives user interactions and sends commands and data back to the App Code.

Details of the commands and logic that we describe in the next paragraphs may change from one database engine to another. The reader is encouraged to look for the appropriate commands for a specific database engine, and to look for additional information and options.

There are multiple choices of database engine (DBMS) that can be used, and installing it is usually a simple procedure. It is necessary to download the software, launch the installer and answer any questions that may be posed (e.g. the installer may ask for installation path, root username and password). After installation, the database engine should be online, and it should also start automatically when the system starts. Database engines come with SQL Client tools, sometimes web-based. The user should look at what SQL Client the particular DBMS has, start the tool and login.

The database server may have more than one database installed (sometimes called instances), corresponding to different schemas and data. For this reason, we must name the database that we want to create and use. The following SQL command creates database dbName.

Create database dbName;

Besides different databases, the database server can have multiple users connecting to it. Connection to a database server requires indication of the user and password. One of the users is the database administrator (dba), a user with extended privileges. As an example, let us connect to a database server as dba (admin), and create user "Mario" with password "secret".

Sqlplus admin/admin
Create user Mario identified as secret;

We need to grant access to a user to be able to access and use a database. For instance, the following SQL commands that are issued using an SQL Client create a database, grant access to Mario to that database, connect, create a toy table "ta", insert a single row in the table and issue a select command to view the contents of the table.

Create database testDatabase;
Grant connect, select, insert to Mario on database testDatabase;
Connect Mario/secret;
Use testDatabase;
Create table ta(a numeric);

Insert into a values(4);
Select * from ta;

The interaction between an application (App Code) and the relational Database is based on DML commands over relations (selects, inserts, deletes and updates). The App Code must be able to connect to the database (wherever it may be), issue SQL commands with variables from the App Code and data received from the UI, retrieve data from the database, using SQL select commands, and handle the data that is retrieved.

Next we describe the interactions between the App Code and the Database. Those interactions are further illustrated using a popular Java (Java™) library for connecting to databases, the JDBC (Java Database Connectivity) (JDBC™).

Connect to the database: In order to connect to any database anywhere, the App Code must specify an IP, a port, a user name and a password. A connection with the server is tried using the IP and port information that were provided. If the connection with the server is successful, connection to the database is tried with the username and password. The App Code becomes connected to the database and can start interacting with it. The following example connects to a postgresSQL™ database named "dbName" running in the machine with IP "192.168.0.101". The connection to the database dbName is to a user named "fred" and the password of fred is "secret".

String url =
"jdbc:postgresql://192.168.0.101/dbName?user=fred&password=secret&ssl=true";

Connection conn = DriverManager.getConnection(url);

In every interaction with the database server, exceptions may happen when the command is not successful. Those exceptions should be handled. The first exception that can happen is during the connection. Perhaps the parameters are wrong, or the server is offline, or there is some internet or wi-fi connection problem.

```
Connection conn=null;
try {
                conn = DriverManager.getConnection(url);
} catch (SQLException ex) {
                DialogBox("Connection unsuccessful");
                ex.printStackTrace();

                Logger.getLogger(ConnectAndRun.class.getName())
                        .log(Level.SEVERE, null, ex);
}
```

Insert, delete, update: simple SQL commands are composed in the App Code by concatenating variable data obtained by the UI and business logic into full SQL commands that operate on the relational data. The following example is a Java method created to insert values into table "ta". Notice the call of method executeUpdate, and the concatenation of an integer parameter "value" into an insert command, in this case using the string concatenation operator "+".

```
void insertValue(int value) {
        try {
                        java.sql.Statement st = conn.createStatement();
                        st.executeUpdate("insert into ta values("+value+ ")");
                } catch (SQLException e) {
                        System.out.println("Failed run statement in JDBC");
                        e.printStackTrace();

                }
}
```

Select: SQL select commands are composed in the App Code by concatenating variable data obtained by the UI and business logic into a full SQL command that operates on the relational data. SELECT commands always retrieve a relation that ends up in a result set. The result set (resultSet) is an in-memory holder of a relation. The resultSet rows can be accessed sequentially using an iterator that reads one row (a tuple) after the previous. For each row that is read, columns (attributes) are accessed by specifying their name (or position). The following is a very simple example. A method is created that returns a string. The string contains the set of values of table ta, separated by white spaces.

The method starts by creating a statement object st. The SELECT query is submitted as a String parameter to the "executeQuery" method of the statement ResultSet rs = st.executeQuery("SELECT * from ta"); The resultset rs is an object that holds the table in-memory. The code then cycles through it using the command while(rs.next()) values += rs.getString("a") + " " ; This command reads one row at a time until all rows are read (while(rs.next())), and retrieves the values of attribute "a" of each row of table "a", concatenating those values to the string called "values", together with a white space. As a result, after all iterations, the string "values" will have all values of table ta, separated by white spaces.

```
String getValues() {

    String values="";

    try {
                java.sql.Statement st = this.conn.createStatement();
                ResultSet rs =
                        st.executeQuery("SELECT * from ta");

                while( rs.next() )
                        values += rs.getString("a") + " " ;

    } catch (SQLException e) {
                System.out.println("Could not create statement in JDBC");
                e.printStackTrace();
    }

    return values;
}
```

Disconnect: a simple disconnection command conn.close() (or a timeout) drops the connection to the database.

7.6. Programming the User Interface

Programming of the user interface and user interactions is usually one of the most important parts of the development of a data application. This book is not about UI programming but, given the importance of the subject to anyone developing a data application, we introduce the subject, show some basic examples of coding, and encourage the reader to search for more information for a particular programming framework he may need to use.

There are many different programming frameworks that can be used, with different syntaxes and tools available to help the programmer. Those frameworks also evolve and some become obsolete quickly. Instead of describing one in detail, we discuss two generic models that are popular regarding user interaction and data management in such frameworks and tools: we denote those as "Web Interactions" (HTML, web servers), and the use of "Rich UI Data Objects". We provide some pseudo-code snippets for the reader to get a quick feeling of how the programming works using those models, you are still required to adapt the pseudo-code. There are also popular programming models, such as MVC ("Model-View-Controller") that are out-of-scope of this book. We encourage the reader to look for further information.

Web Interactions – Web interactions follow a connectionless model, whereby clients submit URLs (Universal Resource Locators) that identify the application server, a request and request parameters. The application server code recognizes the requests, applies any business logic and generates a web page that is rendered inside the client browser. This is the web interaction model used in many data applications.

Figure 55 shows an example of an application that uses the web interaction model. The user must authenticate ("auth.html"). If authentication is successful, the user will see the contents of table a.

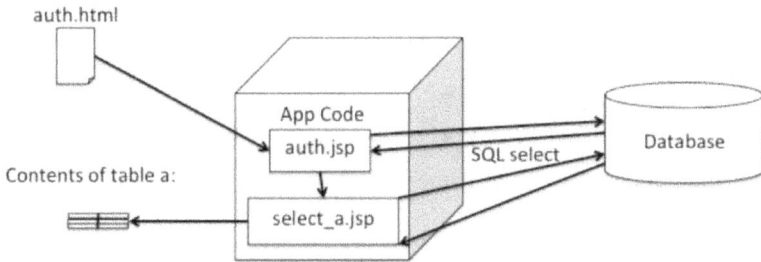

Figure 55. Web Interactions for the Example Table a

In order to install and use an application using web interactions such as this one, it is necessary to install a webserver in the machine holding the App Code. If the reader is not familiar with webservers, we encourage him to search for, download, install and run Apache Tomcat webserver. After the Tomcat webserver is running, look for the directory Webapps (where applications will reside by default), and add a new directory for your application code called TableA. The files that we describe next and which implement application TableA should be placed in the webserver, under the directory TableA. After you have all files of the application installed, test the application by simply opening a web browser and writing the URL http://localhost:8080/TableA/auth.html in the same machine that contains the webserver with the application files. The "localhost" in the URL means the same machine, and 8080 is the default HTTP port (which can be changed in the configuration files of the webserver).

Figure 56 shows the code in page auth.html. It contains a form that uses the method POST. A form is an HTML element that is used to submit requests to the webserver. In this case the request will have two parameters, username and password, that are collected from two input fields that will appear in the browser. The username input field is of type text, and the input field password is of type password, which is hidden text.

auth.html:

```
<html>

<body>
<form action="auth.jsp" method="post">
<p>
User name :<input type="text" name="username" />

<p>
password :<input type="password" name="password" />

<p>
<input type="submit" />


</form>

</body>

</html>
```

Figure 56. Webpage auth.html

Figure 57 shows the output of the code in Figure 56. When the user clicks the "Submit" button, he requests the URL "auth.jsp" with parameters username and password as filled by the user in the corresponding fields.

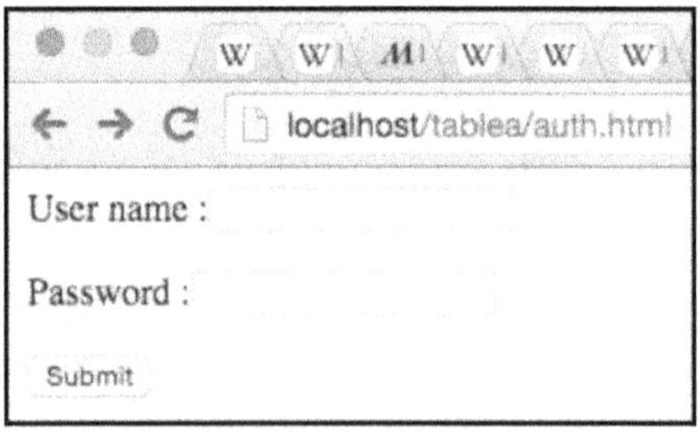

Figure 57. Output of auth.html Form

File "auth.jsp" must retrieve the values of the two parameters and test against a "Users" table in the database. We are supposed to have a Users table, and we insert a test user into the table.

Create table Users(username varchar(25), password varchar(25));
Insert into table Users values("Paul","secret");

We are also supposed to have a table a to read:

Drop table a; // in case the table already exists
Create table a(a1 integer, a2 varchar(25));
Insert into table a values(10,'value1'), (20,'value2');

auth.jsp:

```
<%@ page import ="java.sql.*" %>
<%@ page import ="javax.sql.*" %>
<%

String url =
"jdbc:postgresql://192.168.0.101/dbName?user=fred&password=secret&ssl=tru
e";

String username=request.getParameter("username");
session.putValue("username",username);
String password=request.getParameter("password");

Connection conn=null;

try {
conn = DriverManager.getConnection(url);
 } catch (SQLException ex) {
ex.printStackTrace();
}

try {

        Statement st= con.createStatement();
        ResultSet rs=st.executeQuery("select * from Users where
```

```
                    username="'+username+"'" + " and
                    password='" +username+"'");

        if(rs.next())

        {
            %>
                <jsp:forward page="select_a.jsp"/>
            <%
        }
        else
        {
                %>
                    <jsp:forward page="auth.html"/>
                <%
        }
} catch (SQLException ex) {
ex.printStackTrace();
}

%>
```

select_a.jsp:

```
<%@ page import ="java.sql.*" %>
<%@ page import ="javax.sql.*" %>
<%

String url =
"jdbc:postgresql://192.168.0.101/dbName?user=fred&password=secret&ssl=tru
e";

Connection conn=null;

try {
conn = DriverManager.getConnection(url);
 } catch (SQLException ex) {
ex.printStackTrace();
}
```

```
Statement st= con.createStatement();
ResultSet rs=null;

try {
        rs=st.executeQuery("select * from a");
} catch (SQLException ex) {
ex.printStackTrace();
}


%>

 <TABLE BORDER="1">
        <TR>
          <TH></TH>
          <TH>Attribute 1</TH>
          <TH> Attribute 2</TH>
</TR>
        <% while(rs.next()){ %>
<TR>
                <TD> <%= resultset.getInteger(1) %></td>
                <TD> <%= resultset.getString(2) %></TD>
</TR>
        <% } %>
      </TABLE>
```

Data-rich objects – We call "Rich UI Data Objects" a set of techniques that some programming frameworks provide to create functionality-rich objects that are configured to retrieve, display and interact with data from databases. At programming time, users configure parameters needed by the objects to manage the data and interact with the users through a user interface. Users also configure and/or program the application dynamics, with windows or frames that open and close as a result of user actions, and contain the objects that manage data. When the resulting application is ran, the objects will handle database access and user interactions. The frameworks offering "Rich UI Data Objects" are also most often associated with integrated development environments (IDE) that allow the user to design interfaces by dragging and dropping components such as windows, buttons and rich objects to window frames, defining the layout of the application by moving the visual objects, and configuring both those objects and the application flow (navigation between screens).

Next we show a simple Swing (Java™ Foundation Classes) application that uses a JFrame and a JTable to display the data from table "Objects". The application retrieves data from the database using the a retrieveObjects() method of the RetrieveObjects class. This method uses the same connection and statement issuing approach that we defined in the previous examples. However, this time it places the contents of the resultSet inside a two-dimensional array with code and object name. This array that contains the table data is returned. The ShowObjectsTable class extends a JFrame, creating a window that will display the objects as a table. The table object is built with an instance of a JTable class, which has a title and receives two arrays as input to the constructor. The first array contains the data, which is the multidimensional array of objects, and the second array contains the column titles for the table.

```
import javax.swing.JFrame;
import javax.swing.JScrollPane;
import javax.swing.JTable;
import javax.swing.SwingUtilities;

public class RetrieveObjects
{

    public Object[][] retrieveObjects()
    {

                Object[][] data = new String[][];
String url =
"jdbc:postgresql://192.168.0.101/dbName?user=fred&password=secret&ssl=true";

                Connection conn=null;
```

```
            try {
                    conn = DriverManager.getConnection(url);
            } catch (SQLException ex) {
                    ex.printStackTrace();
            }


            Statement st= conn.createStatement();
            ResultSet rs=null;

            try {
                    rs=st.executeQuery("select * from objects");

                    int i=0;
                    while(rs.next()){
                     data[i][0]=rs.getInteger(1).toString();
                     data[i][1]=rs.getString(2);
                     i++;
            }

            } catch (SQLException ex) {
                    ex.printStackTrace();
            }

    return data;
    }
}

public class ShowObjectsTable extends JFrame
{
   public ShowObjectsTable()
   {
     //attributes
     String[] attributes = new String[] {
        "Code", "Name"
     };


   RetrieveObjects ro=new RetrieveObjects();
```

```
        Object[][] data = ro.retrieveObjects();

        JTable table = new JTable(data, attributes);

        this.add(new JScrollPane(table));

        this.setTitle("Show Objects Table");
        this.setDefaultCloseOperation(JFrame.EXIT_ON_CLOSE);
        this.pack();
        this.setVisible(true);
    }

    public static void main(String[] args)
    {
        SwingUtilities.invokeLater(new Runnable() {
          @Override
          public void run() {
             new ShowObjectsTable();
          }
        });
    }
}
```

The next code creates a simple form receiving user input data and, when the user clicks the "Insert" button, the data consisting of code and object name is inserted into the table "objects". The executable class GetUserInput extends class JFrame, to create a window where the interaction with the user happens. Method "main" sets the window to visible. The constructor of GetUserInput calls three methods. The first one (initializeComponents) initializes the components that the window will show, the second one (connectToDB) connects to the database, and the third one sets the size of the window.

The initializeComponents method initializes text fields that will receive the code and the object name from the user. These text fields also have labels next to them. This method also initializes a JButton

(JButtonInsert), which is the one the user presses to insert data into the objects table. In order to instruct the JButtonInsert button to insert the object data into the database, a listener jButtonInsert.addActionListener is created. The listener responds to the button press by calling the insert() method. The insert method constructs an SQL code to insert the data into the table.

Code :

```
import java.sql.Connection;
import java.sql.DriverManager;
import java.sql.PreparedStatement;
import java.sql.ResultSet;
import javax.swing.JFrame;
import javax.swing.JOptionPane;

public class GetUserInput extends JFrame {


// Variables declaration
private javax.swing.JButton jButtonInsert;
private javax.swing.JLabel jLabelCode;
private javax.swing.JLabel jLabelObjectName;

private javax.swing.JScrollPane jScrollPane;

private javax.swing.JTextArea jTextArea;
private javax.swing.JTextField jTextFieldCode;
private javax.swing.JTextField jTextFieldObjectName;
// End of variables declaration



/* Driver for Database */

String url =
"jdbc:postgresql://192.168.0.101/dbName?user=fred&password=secret&ssl=tru
e";

Connection conn=null;
```

```
public GetUserInput () {

initializeComponents();
connectToDB();
setSize(600,400);

}

public void insertInObjectsTable()
{
try
{
preparedStatement=c.prepareStatement("insert into objects values(?,?)");
preparedStatement.setObject(1, jTextField1.getText());
preparedStatement.setObject(2, jTextField2.getText());
preparedStatement.executeUpdate();

}catch(Exception e){
JOptionPane.showMessageDialog(this, e.getMessage());

}

}

public void ConnectToDB()
{
try {
conn = DriverManager.getConnection(url);
 } catch (SQLException ex) {
ex.printStackTrace();
}
catch(Exception e){
JOptionPane.showMessageDialog(this, e.getMessage());
}
}

private void initializeComponents() {
```

```
jLabelCode = new javax.swing.JLabel();
jLabelObjectName = new javax.swing.JLabel();

jTextFieldCode = new javax.swing.JTextField();
jTextFieldObjectName = new javax.swing.JTextField();

jButtonInsert = new javax.swing.JButton();

jLabelCode.setText("Code :");
getContentPane().add(jLabelCode);
jLabelCode.setBounds(20, 40, 70, 10);

jLabelObjectName.setText("Object Name:");
getContentPane().add(jLabelObjectName);
jLabelObjectName.setBounds(20, 70, 50, 10);

setDefaultCloseOperation(javax.swing.WindowConstants.EXIT_ON_CLOSE);
getContentPane().setLayout(null);


jButtonInsert.setText("Insert");

/* Add button Listener to insert objects into the database*/

jButtonInsert.addActionListener(new java.awt.event.ActionListener() {

        public void actionPerformed(java.awt.event.ActionEvent evt) {
            jButtonInsertActionPerformed(evt);
            }
            });

        getContentPane().add(jButtonInsert);
        jButtonInsert.setBounds(90, 200, 170, 23);

        pack();
    }

// call insert when Insert button is pressed
private void
```

```
jButtonInsertActionPerformed(java.awt.event.ActionEvent evt) {
        insertInObjectsTable();

}

public static void main(String args[]) {
        new GetUserInput ().setVisible(true);
}
```

The above pseudo-code snippets and descriptions are just a short introduction to programming UI for data applications. The most important purpose of this introduction was to give the reader initial insight so that he can explore himself the languages and frameworks.

7.7. Importing and Exporting Data

Importing and exporting data from databases allows you to load or dump between operating system files and relations in databases. You can for instance export data from some database system into a file, bring it to another place and import it back into another database.

Database tools frequently include import and export UI tools that you can use. Alternatively, you can import and export data using SQL commands that we show next.

We will use a very simple example to show you how to import data. There are usually some minor difficulties with this process. You may have difficulties with absolute paths and permissions, depending on the database server you will be using.

First, create table "objects" in the database server:

Create table objects(code integer, b varchar2(25));

Now create comma-separated values file objects.csv with the following lines:

1,Curtains 2,Chair

After this is done, load the data into the database using the data loading or importing SQL command. You will need to search for the adequate command depending on the database server. MySQL™ would be:

load data infile "path/objects.csv" into table objects
        fields terminated by "," lines terminated by "\r\n";

In a postgreSQL™ database server, all you need to do is write the code:

copy objects FROM 'path/objects.csv'

Exporting data into a file is also easy. In a postgreSQL™ database server, all you need to do is run the command:

copy (select * from objects) to 'path/objectsB.csv';

Each database server has its own mechanisms to import and export data, and it is possible to export only the data or the schema and data, as a set of SQL commands. The reader is encouraged to search for the appropriate mechanism depending on the database server.

Page intentionally left blank

Pedro Furtado

Page intentionally left blank

8. References

[1] Codd, E. F. (1970). "A relational model of data for large shared data banks". Communications of the ACM 13 (6): 377. doi:10.1145/362384.362685.

[2] Codd, E.F. "Further Normalization of the Data Base Relational Model". IBM Research Report RJ909 (August 31, 1971). Republished in Randall J. Rustin (ed.), Data Base Systems: Courant Computer Science Symposia Series 6. Prentice-Hall, 1972.

[3] Codd, E. F. (1982). "Relational database: A practical foundation for productivity". Communications of the ACM 25 (2): 109. doi:10.1145/358396.358400.

[4] Chen, Peter (March 1976). "The Entity-Relationship Model - Toward a Unified View of Data". ACM Transactions on Database Systems 1 (1): 9–36. doi:10.1145/320434.320440.

[5] "Database System Concepts", Sixth Edition. By Avi Silberschatz, Henry F. Korth, S. Sudarshan. McGraw-Hill, ISBN 0-07-352332-1.

[6] Database management systems (3. ed.). By Raghu Ramakrishnan, Johannes Gehrke. McGraw-Hill 2003, ISBN 978-0-07-115110-8, pp. I-XXXII, 1-1065

[7] Principles of Database and Knowledge-Base Systems, Volume I. By Jeffrey D. Ullman. Computer Science Press 1988, ISBN 0-7167-8158-1

[8] "Fundamentals of Database Systems" by R. Elmasri and S. Navathe. Benjamin/Cummings 1994, ISBN 0-8053-1748-1.

[9] "Foundations of Databases" by Serge Abiteboul, Richard Hull and Victor Vianu. Addison-Wesley 1995, ISBN 0-201-53771-0.

[10] SQL: Practical Guide for Developers (The Practical Guides) Morgan Kaufmann; 1 edition (August 15, 2005). ISBN-13: 978-0122205316.

[11] SQL: The Complete Reference, Second Edition, by James R. Groff and Paul N. Weinberg. McGraw-Hill/Osborne, 0-07-222817-2.

[12] King, Gavin; Christian, Bauer (November 24, 2006), Java Persistence with Hibernate (Second ed.), Manning Publications, p. 880, ISBN 1-932394-88-5.

[13] Hibernate.org website [last accessed on Jan, 2015].

[14] Schwaber, Ken; Beedle, Mike (2002). Agile software development with Scrum. Prentice Hall. ISBN 0-13-067634-9.

[15] Grady Booch, James Rumbaugh, Ivar Jacobson, "Unified Modeling Language User Guide", The (2 ed.). Addison-Wesley. 2005. p. 496. ISBN 0321267974.

[16] www.uml.org [last accessed on Jan, 2015].

Database Design and Development of Applications

Pedro Furtado

www.ingramcontent.com/pod-product-compliance
Lightning Source LLC
Chambersburg PA
CBHW070723220326

41598CB00024BA/3270